Coasting around Scotland

To Vivienne and Ken

With Best Wishes

Nick Fairweather

Coasting around Scotland

Nicholas Fairweather

Cualann Press

ISBN 0 9535036 8 2

First Edition 2002

British Library Cataloguing in Publication Data. A catalogue record of this book is available at the British Library.

Printed by Bell & Bain, Glasgow

Published by:

Cualann Press, 6 Corpach Drive, Dunfermline, KY12 7XG, Scotland
Tel/Fax 01383 733724
Email: cualann@btinternet.com Website: www.cualann.co.uk

Biographical Note

Nicholas Fairweather, born in Sussex in 1945, was brought up in the south of England by Scottish parents. Love of the Scottish landscape was fostered by childhood summer holidays spent in the Cairngorms where he climbed his first 'Munro' at the age of eleven. He graduated with a degree in Microbiology from University College London in 1963 and worked in scientific research and development for a London-based pharmaceutical company for the next eight years. After taking a Diploma in Careers Guidance, Nicholas moved to Scotland. He now lives in Edinburgh with his wife and two children, working as a guidance manager with Careers Scotland and finding some time to pursue his love of the hills and 'hatred' of golf.

Acknowledgements

Thanks are due to Caledonian MacBrayne for enabling some of the photography for *Coasting around Scotland*.

I am grateful to Robin Harper for taking time from his busy schedule to write the Foreword, Seán Bradley for his advice and encouragement and Andrew Simpson for contributing photographs.

I am indebted to my parents and brothers for helping develop my love of the Scottish landscape and to Dorothy, Joanna and Gareth for their support throughout the cycling expeditions and the writing of the book.

Contents

Crossing the Borders 161

Illustrations

Colour Section

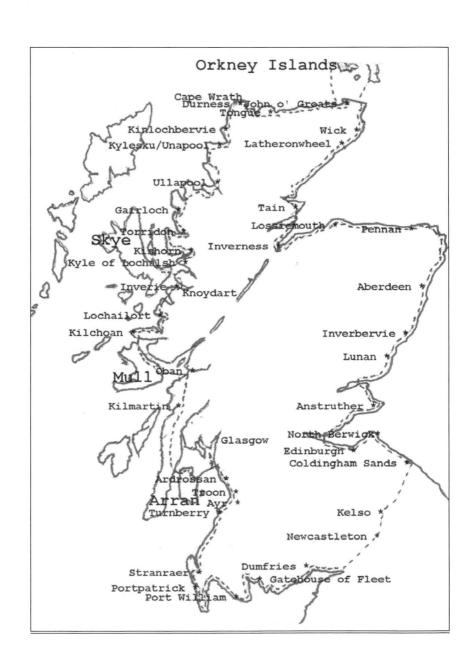

Foreword

Dear Reader,

Get out a map: either a one-glance map of Scotland or, probably better, one of these big road maps. Check to see if it has the cycling routes in it. Of course, it won't have – but it is about time that our road maps also included as many cycling and walking tracks as space allows.

Nicholas Fairweather was inspired by many things when he wrote *Coasting around Scotland*, but I think that his comment on the simple experience of accomplishing his tour on his own says it all. Somehow, being alone heightens senses and lifts the soul. This is a book that should inspire not only cyclists but also anybody with the beginnings of a sense of the extraordinary drama and beauty of Scotland's coastline and a feeling for the entire history of Scotland. Nicholas has a sure touch in recounting his experience and understanding of everything from the geology to the social history of Scotland. He has a delightful propensity for absorbing an immense amount of detail and then recounting it in terms that anyone could appreciate, enjoy and understand. Nicholas's brief history of Scotland at the end of this book should be read before starting the journey with him round Scotland's coastline.

I have read quite a few travel books and I have come to the conclusion that if the traveller has a sense of humour, is of an inquisitive nature and has an adventurous empathy with his journey, then usually all these urges will be rewarded. This is certainly more than reflected in Nicholas Fairweather's journal of his off-and-on, four-and-a-half-year, one-and-a-half-thousand-mile trip round Scotland. There is hardly a mile of the journey where Nicholas has not picked up a legend or some local history, or been able in graphic terms to describe one or other aspect of the extraordinary beauty of our coastline. I have personally seen much of what he has described and have found that, not only have his descriptions touched my heart, but they have also instilled a deep and immediate longing to revisit the scenes he has portrayed so vividly. Whether it be the Carrick coast, Stac Pollaidh, Suilven or the wilds of the northernmost parts of Scotland, he has an equally deft touch. In a very few words, he captures the enormous physical presence of these ancient geological formations.

Look out for the encounters with a dead sheep (or at least an apparently dead sheep), with less than community-spirited cyclists and drivers and the many necessary journeys by boat and ferry.

If you are a cyclist, this book should inspire you to make full use of the Sustrans paths that have now been created all over Scotland. Of course, you are unlikely to have quite the same adventures as Nicholas Fairweather because you won't be humping your bike over almost unmarked pedestrian tracks or through woods or across lochs where you have to phone up and hire a boat several days in advance. However, you will be able to share the joys of our extraordinary Scottish countryside, free of the noise and threat of motorised traffic and pretty sure in the knowledge that wherever you end up, you will be able to cycle to a Youth Hostel or Bed and Breakfast that is affordable. These are the places where your adventures may well start. It's clear from Nicholas's experiences that there is much to be learnt about human nature from staying in such places that does not come to those people who are able to insulate themselves behind the service levels of our four star hotels. I will not say more on this subject. Read, learn, inwardly digest – and enjoy.

For the non-cyclist, the lessons that Nicholas learnt on his journey as a cyclist might confirm the less adventurous among us in the view that even if it took us another eight to fifteen years to get round Scotland's coastline on foot, it might be an easier way to do it. But don't forget the huge physical achievement. It only took Nicholas thirty-five days – in other words, a super-fit person intent on following the same route might be able to do it in a summer vacation. I am certain that the sheer enjoyment that jumps out from every page of this book is due to the fact that Nicholas decided to take it a bit at a time.

This book is not an account of a cycling marathon. It recounts one person's sensitive and perceptive and good-humoured reactions to the beauty and history of Scotland's coastline as it unfolded to him on his travels with a bicycle.

Robin Harper MSP

Part 1

Cycling on the Western Shore

Shieldaig, Loch Torridon

Getting started

I spent an hour sitting on the rocks at the end of Ardnamurchan watching storm clouds drag their curtain of rain over distant Coll and Tiree. What a view! What a goal-scoring sense of achievement!

It had taken me a long time to reach those rocks: thirty-eight years in fact since my first taste of childhood freedom on my shiny green and yellow Dawes with drop handlebars and plastic drinking-bottle. I had dreamt of great journeys as I cycled along the country lanes of Sussex wearing my matching hand-knitted green sweater with the horizontal yellow stripe – racing colours but cosy as well. Five trousers' sizes later, I decided to start pedalling whilst there was still some energy left in my legs. My Dawes had been replaced by a twenty-one gear, purple chunky-tyred Shogun mountain bike. The childish enthusiasm was still there: with much more of a wobble.

Starting at Portpatrick, my journey up the west coast of Scotland at first followed coastal roads and tracks over Arran and Mull to Ardnamurchan. I cycled round Knoydart, hitching lifts across the lochs of Nevis and Hourn and then took the Glenelg ferry to Skye. There were more tracks to follow from Torridon, another boat trip to Ullapool before a hard pedal through Assynt to Sandwood Bay and my arrival at Cape Wrath. Although I had planned to end my coastal exploration at the Cape, one look along the gallery of cliffs that map out Scotland's northern edge meant a return to pedalling some time later, crossing over to Orkney before heading south, through the forest sands of Culbin and Tentsmuir, and home to Edinburgh. The full coastal round was eventually completed by reaching St Abb's Head and crossing the Borders to Dumfries and the Mull of Galloway.

I had taken my time on the journey to enjoy the finest coastal scenery in Europe – some four and a half years in fact – from October 1992 to June 1997. Cycling the fifteen hundred miles around the edge of Scotland had taken thirty-five days. Of course there had been a lot of planning in between the weeklong trips and some hard winter evenings were spent staring at Ordnance Survey maps with only a glass of Merlot to keep me company.

This is a book for those who enjoy reading about or exploring the outdoors and the rugged beauty of Scotland's coast. It is not a tale of macho mountain-biking, although some of the cross-country routes were wearying to say the least. It is written to celebrate this wild coastline of ours and perhaps encourage those who enjoy a pedal to visit some very special places.

The well-travelled bicycle on the harbour wall at Granton

Portpatrick to Turnberry: 19 September 1992

I had always known that reaching the starting point was going to be difficult. Just getting me, the bike and family packed into the car in Edinburgh seemed to take forever. I needed to leave early to get down to Galloway in time to make the most of the day, but there were the usual delays caused by packing, loading, shopping, locking, unlocking and 'we-might-as-well-have-lunch-first' before we finally got away. So the first hazard of the journey was to negotiate the afternoon traffic in Morningside. Doubts soon set in about the wisdom of the whole trip, doubts possibly shared by an elderly Edinburgh driver who, as I drew up next to him at traffic lights, took the trouble to wind down his window and shout 'Fool'. Did he know something about my plans or was he referring to my attempts to overtake him whilst he carried out a two-mile parking manoeuvre?

It was a silent, white-knuckled drive out of Lothian, especially when my children decided to confront the rising tension in the car with the obvious question. 'Do you really have to do this cycling, Dad?' Even Dorothy, who had agreed to drop me off in Portpatrick, began to wonder whether her husband was fit enough to cope with the car journey, let alone cycling at the end of it. My mouth was too dry to answer but by now I knew that, come rain, wind or darkness, I was 'for the off''.

What a relief to reach the Galloway coast even though it was five o'clock in the evening and raining. Portpatrick reminded me of coastal villages that I had visited in parts of Pembrokeshire and Cornwall: narrow main street winding down the steep hillside to the small stone-built harbour. It could have been Dylan Thomas's *Llareggubb*, 'to begin at the beginning', a natural starting point, not only for me but also for those walking the Southern Upland Way. Even Saint Patrick himself is renowned for crossing to Ireland from here, usually in just one stride, and often with his head tucked under his arm. The village was also once the main sailing point to Ireland until the service went to Stranraer when steamboats needed a larger harbour.

Ready to leave: the author at Portpatrick

It was just after five o'clock, darkness, 'starry and bible black', only a few hours away, when I started pedalling the fifty-two miles to Ayr. Leaving the harbour, I cycled back up the hill and headed west along the A77 before turning north towards Stranraer. Despite the rain and fumes from the heavy traffic, it was good to be travelling at last. Where did all these cars come from and where were they going to at this time of day? It took me just under an hour to reach Stranraer, a busy place, full of traffic lights and perhaps not looking its best on this grey evening. But it is a fine setting on the shores of Loch Ryan, the most southerly of the west coast's thirty large sea lochs, and there is a grand promenade road that leads out of town towards Girvan. The sight of the bay curving round the foot of the low-lying coastal hills ended any remaining doubts about setting out on my journey.

When I saw the number of ferries on Loch Ryan, I realised why there was so much traffic on the roads. A P&O Sea Cat ferry was gliding down the loch to dock alongside the larger boats at one of the two ferry terminals. It was strange to see so much activity amid the quiet, rolling countryside of farms and moorland. The road stays close to the beach and there were views across silvered waters, west to the hills or Rhins of Galloway and north to the narrow exit to the open sea. Just before reaching the end of the loch, the road turns inland and up into Glen App. It climbs slowly, or rather, I climbed slowly up through woodlands and onto the coastal hills, autumn-coloured in the light and dark browns of bracken and heather. I stopped for a time before resuming pedalling on what now seemed to be an endless uphill grind. A red

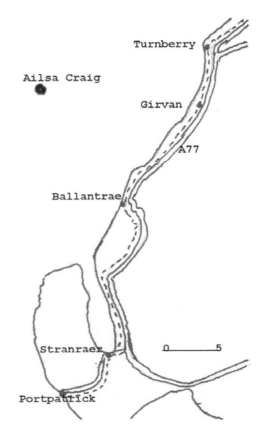

deer came crackling through the undergrowth, right up to the roadside and then, startled by the sight of me, fled back into the forest. This was one of the many times on my coastal journey when I enjoyed the closeness of the surrounding landscape which is invisibly screened from the car traveller.

It had taken me some time to cycle the five miles up Glen App. The overcast evening sky had become decidedly gloomy by the time I finally reached the crest of the hill. I could now see the lights of the small village of Ballantrae several hundred feet below me, tucked into a corner of the coastline. To the north-west, the one-thousand-foot, grey sea-mountain, Ailsa Craig, rose steeply out of the water. This large, impressive island rock, known locally as Paddy's Milestone, (because it is half way between Glasgow and Belfast) seemed to loom even larger in the evening light. The road now dropped steeply down to the coast and I enjoyed an all too brief, but exhilarating, descent, especially as I negotiated the bends near the bottom. Although the hurtling was short, the hurting of tired muscles began as I made my way along the shore. Thoughts of reaching Ayr that night disappeared into the dusk.

The road remained close to the shore and large sea-smoothed rocks on the beach formed ghostly pale shapes in the darkening gloom. They occasionally appeared to move like stretching seals against the background of white-crested waves. This is a lonely stretch of the Carrick coast road where an earlier Mr Bean, Sawney Bean, and his family lived in a cave and dined on passing travellers. Slightly further on at Games Loup, another local worthy, Sir John Cathcart of Carleton Castle, pushed a succession of his brides over the cliffs to their deaths. He must have been a good talker because he got to Mrs Cathcart number eight before she managed to do the shoving. The road has had more than its fair share of spooky characters although one local bank manager, Henry Ewing Torbet (1912-1983), obviously enjoyed the ambience of the area. He escaped from the ties of domestic life and day-to-day banking by moving into a cave across the road from the bank. No wonder I was just glad, after a further eleven long miles, to see the lights of Girvan shining out across Woodland Bay. It took me a long time to reach them.

My limited experience of cycling at night had been in relatively well-lit city streets and it came as a shock to discover just how black the night could be when I left behind the street lamps of Girvan. My front bicycle lamp provided only a small circle of light, about three feet in diameter, leaving the rest of the road in total darkness. Light rain began to fall, and for some reason it became even darker when the road moved away from the coast. I could now see nothing except my little circular pool of light which I aimed carefully at the white line along the side. This was the only way to work out where I was on the road. An oncoming vehicle, headlights blazing, came racing towards me out of the darkness. It seemed to be taking up most, if not the whole width. The closer it got, the more convinced I became that it was coming straight at me along the centre of the road. Slowly I began to realise that, if the car was in the middle and we were on a collision course, then I was also travelling along the centre line. What if my small pool of light was picking out the white line in the middle and not the sideline? I imagined the shaken driver explaining to the police that 'the fool just cycled straight under my wheels, officer'. As my powers of deduction were beginning to speed up, I realised that I only had a matter of seconds to test my 'wrong line theory'. I had to turn sharp left immediately. If I had been following the centre line, I would cross quite a distance before I hit the kerb.

The car did not even slow down as it passed me. Maybe the driver was a little puzzled as to why that cyclist had so suddenly and purposefully decided to topple over into the ditch. Maybe these mountain bike riders can't resist the rugged ground even in the dark?

When I had climbed out of the ditch, I paused for a brief curse before starting to cycle again. It was back to staring at my lit circle until I reached the sanctuary of the street lamps at the Turnberry junction. About an hour later than I should have, I finally came to the conclusion that there was little point in continuing on the coast road in the dark. I turned off my route and headed for Maybole. A combination of tiredness and the isolating darkness convinced me that

I was cycling uphill all the time now. On one occasion, the bike began to free-wheel downhill as I walked at its side. I eventually reached Maybole where Dorothy met me with the car and gave me a lift to Ayr. Tomorrow I would return to Turnberry. I vowed to avoid all night-time cycling in future.

Turnberry to Ayr

Next morning, heavy rain led to an unhurried return to the coast road at the junction just south of Turnberry to set off once again for Ayr. For the next mile or so, the road runs straight and flat, passing the landscaped greenery of the Turnberry golf courses. Television coverage has made the red-roofed Turnberry Hotel, terraced lawns and putting greens, a familiar landmark. I could imagine the temptation, following the consumption of a few malts, to hit a golf ball from the front entrance of the hotel, across the road onto the famous Ailsa course. It was here at the Open Championship in 1977 that I watched Jack Nicklaus and Tom Watson partner each other on the practice round before they went on to play in that epic championship which was only decided by a putt on the last green. In those days, the practice rounds were less formally organised and the crowds had the chance to walk alongside the great and the good. Towards the end of that practice day, I joined a small group of spectators to follow Tom Weiskopf and David Graham, two of the many top golfers gathered for The Open. They seemed to be enjoying the warm evening sunshine, chatting to us and playing golf of a standard, which to me as a hack golfer, seemed close to relaxed perfection. It took about five holes for me to think of a question to ask. Our chat was all too brief:

Fairweather: 'Do you think that Tony Jacklin will ever win the Open again?'

Weiskopf: 'It depends on whether he wants to enough.'

Fairweather: 'Umm, yes.' Pause. 'I suppose so.'

I left the course shortly afterwards feeling strangely moved not only by the profundity of wise Tom's observation but by the mind-numbing dumbness of mine.

I have long since abandoned all hopes of achieving that state of 'relaxed perfection' on a golf course and instead try my best to cope with my own deeply personal game of 'anxiety golf'. It was a relief to be cycling again and I was content to stay on the road rather than worrying about driving onto it.

The A719 is hidden from the sea by high sand dunes that shape the golf course. The only glimpse of the water was at the village of Maidens. Beyond the fine beach and numerous caravans of the village, the road turned inland and up onto the coastal headlands. The hedgerows were thick with bramble bushes and the chance to eat the ripened fruit was an ideal excuse for frequent stops on my way up into the Carrick foothills.

I understand that at certain tides it is possible to walk along the shore from Turnberry to Culzean Bay and avoid a detour inland. Instead, however, I followed the road through wooded countryside towards Maybole, before branching off to the left at Pennyglen and heading back towards Ayr and the sea. This route also allowed me to test out the 'Electric Brae', an optical illusion which makes a downhill stretch of road look as if it is going upwards. It is a nicely understated phenomenon; a simple sign marks the brae and there is not an interpretive centre in sight. Even though I had been here before, I still thought that I would have to pedal uphill rather than free-wheel down the brae. On reaching the brow of this 'downhill', there was a great view of the Ayrshire coastline displaying headlands of green fields. To the south was the sweep of Culzean Bay, and westwards across the open sea, the cone of Ailsa Craig and the distant outlines of the Mull of Kintyre and Ireland. The clouds were massing out at sea and a storm was making its way up the Firth of Clyde towards the Isle of Arran. Once passed, the sun came out again, and Culzean Castle, until now hidden in the greyness of the hills, was lit up, appearing to grow out of the cliffs.

The road stays high up on the headlands for the next few miles, views stretching over the ruined castle at Dunure and across the Firth to the rugged mountains of Arran. I reached the gates of 'Wonderland', the renamed Butlins holiday camp on the Heads of Ayr. The sign at the entrance stated that 'Wonderland welcomes campers and day tourists.' And anyone? Shortly after passing the camp, the road leaves its cliff-top route across the Heads of Ayr and drops down to the seaside.

Heads of Ayr

I made my way through the lawns and putting greens of Ayr and onto the broad promenade which edges the wide expanse of sand. This 'honest toun', wrapped in memories of Robert Burns, has managed to retain its dignity whilst continuing to attract day-trippers. The tide was out and several people taking the evening air wandered along the white stretch of flattened beach. Two dogs raced across the sand in ever-widening circles until all of a sudden they both appeared to lose interest at the same time and retreated to their owners' heels. In contrast, back on the promenade, bored-looking male youths patrolled in loud cars – all thumping bass and exhaust with the occasional handbrake turn to squeal the wheels. Yes, this is the place to be if you want to burn rubber and listen to the lapping of the airwaves.

'Auld Ayr, wham ne'er a town surpasses, for honest men an' bonnie lasses'.

But no mention of Vauxhall Vivas.

Ayr to Ardrossan

I left early next day whilst the sun was still burning off the autumn chill of the morning and made my way northwards along the main road to the neighbouring town of Prestwick. I was surprised to discover later that this ancient burgh, although much smaller than Ayr, still has a bigger population than any other town that I would visit on the rest of the west coast.

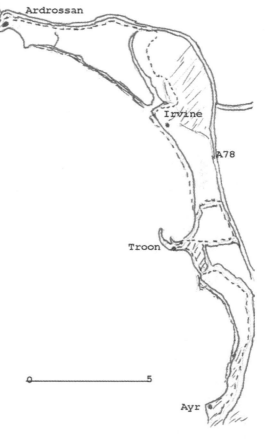

I cycled past the sign for 'Bruce's Well', familiar from previous visits to Ayr. It is strange how there are certain signs that you always notice and this was one that I never missed. I used to wonder whether it was a statement of health or a friendly way of naming a local monument. Perhaps there was a 'Malcolm's Poorly' sign somewhere.

As the main road leaves the town, the two other reasons for Prestwick's fame come into view. On the left, between the road and the sea, is the tumbled greenery of Prestwick golf course which used to host the Open Championship. Sadly, in 1925, there were some crowd control problems when spectators mobbed the Championship leader – hooligan fans even then – and the tournament was never held there again. The place on the other side of the road, Prestwick Airport, would, however, have welcomed some crowd control problems. While the terminal building architecture looked authentic enough and there were acres of runway, the occasional plane would have added that extra touch of credibility. The third reason for Prestwick's fame is that it is the only place in Britain that Elvis Presley visited – allegedly.

It was turning out to be a beautiful day and I stopped to look at the view of Arran across the rolling green baize of the golf course. I almost took the definitive calendar photograph but decided to wait until I got closer and snap an even better one from Troon. Sharp and clear stood the tops of the island's mountain ridge which was circled in a wreath of low-lying cloud. In his book *In Scotland Again*, H V Morton describes Arran as 'some magic island that had been towed into the Firth of Clyde from the Golden Age'. Arran's jagged mountain crest certainly does look out of place surrounded by the gentler landscape of the Ayrshire and Kintyre coastlines. Perhaps it is just a clever piece of theatre scenery because it can disappear off stage quickly enough. Arran is only the first of a series of majestic islands and mountains that make the west-coast seascapes so memorable. Later on there would be silhouettes of Rum and Skye before the stage-struck Sutherland mountains of Suilven, Canisp and Quinag crawl onto the northern mainland.

The road to Troon travels inland, passing through woodlands before entering the neat and fashionable town which is besieged by golf courses and marinas. The low morning sunlight highlighted the soft contours of a golf course and I stopped to watch a red cardigan swinging a club. From a distance, it looked like a relaxing way to spend a holiday morning but if you're actually playing, you are likely to be in the middle of some mental or physical breakdown and wondering why you didn't go for a simple cycle ride instead, and anyway, what's that fool waiting there for? Go on, off with you on your bike and let me concentrate on hating this game!

I followed a road down to the sea only to find that Arran had been towed away into the haze, and with it, my photographic masterpiece. Still, here was an elegant part of town with a crescent of lawns and flowerbeds and a sense of dignified 'Troon on the Green' until it came to an abrupt end amongst the sheds and shackles of the harbour.

I hadn't bothered to bring a map – if you can't find your own way from Ayr to Ardrossan, then what chance Cape Wrath? I soon became confused by Troon's road system. All roads seemed to lead back into town and away from the sea. I realised later that Troon is built on a peninsula where the bays of Ayr and Irvine meet and most of the roads run east to west rather than, as a mapless visitor might expect, from north to south. I asked in a cycle shop for local route maps but directions were all that were on offer. Why is it that I never listen to directions until my guide has described the first three miles and we're 'turning left at the shop with the large inflatable pig in the window.' Maybe I'm too busy establishing eye contact and smiling appreciatively at the clarity and precision of the explanation to take in anything after 'turn right outside the shop and … ' I also become very bored listening to directions and attempt to hide this with a mask of grateful nodding. So with the attention span of a coffee advert viewer, I usually find that I've asked someone who has the verbal stamina for a description of the 'Ascent of Man'. Sometimes, if I'm really lost, I'll try to get a brief rerun, starting with the only bit I've heard. 'So if I turn right when I leave the shop, I go where again?' The only problem is that it is even more tedious the second time and once again the inflatable pig is the only highlight. I left the shop with an understanding smile, turned right and was lost. I kept a wary eye out for a certain shop window. I wasn't surprised, half an hour later, to cycle past a sign saying 'Welcome to Troon'!

I did finally escape from the town by heading off down the coast road through neighbouring Barassie and onto the beach at Irvine Bay. The tide was out, the sun was out, and even Arran emerged from the haze to enjoy the view. It was good to get away from the traffic and there was a sense of freedom about cycling on the sand. However, it was hard work trying to find the easiest surface to cross because it is almost impossible to make any progress if the sand is dry and powdery. It was also too soft near the water and I tried to stay on the high tide line where the crust was firm. Despite all my beached euphoria, I was relieved to reach the tarmac at Irvine, even though the road into town took me past the grim car park architecture of the local Magnum Sports Centre.

The parked security van on the other side of the street reminded me that all was well with the world because 'Securicor cares'. It's these little comforting messages that have kept me going through the last fifteen years. While we may be cultivating the creed of competitive greed, there are many pillars of commerce that want us to know that they're looking after us. Only a few days earlier, I had received a letter from my 'friend for life' and fifteen pounds seemed a paltry sum to pay for this treasured correspondence!

Just outside the railway station, I spotted, high up on a lamp-post, what I thought was a sign for a cycle track. A little extra detail telling me which one went northwards would have been helpful; no doubt the people in the corner shop under the shadow of the signs would be able to tell me. 'What cycle track'? Well clearly here was a business failing to capitalise on a market opportunity. No sales of 'biker burgers' or 'track snacks', so I settled for some peanuts and chocolate to guard against excessive weight loss. I crossed the river twice and cycled into a builder's yard before finally leaving Irvine. When I did find the cycle track, it was a good one, crossing open moorland with still some colour in the heather. The track then narrowed to a path, forcing its way through overgrown marshland reeds and hedgerows before emerging, all too suddenly, onto the busy A78 dual carriageway between Kilwinning and Stevenston. There seemed no way to avoid following this trunk road to Ardrossan.

Ardrossan is a small town with a big harbour and numerous traffic lights; most of these seem to favour the colour red, especially when you're in a car and late for the ferry. I cycled down to the ferry terminal and sat on the harbour wall to bask in the warm sunshine and gaze at the view across the Clyde towards its beautiful isle. My sense of achievement and pleasure at having reached this far was all too soon overtaken by an impatience for further travel. I longed to cross over to Arran and wished that I could have caught the afternoon ferry rather than wait till morning.

The next morning in Ardrossan for me was cold, windy and eight months later.

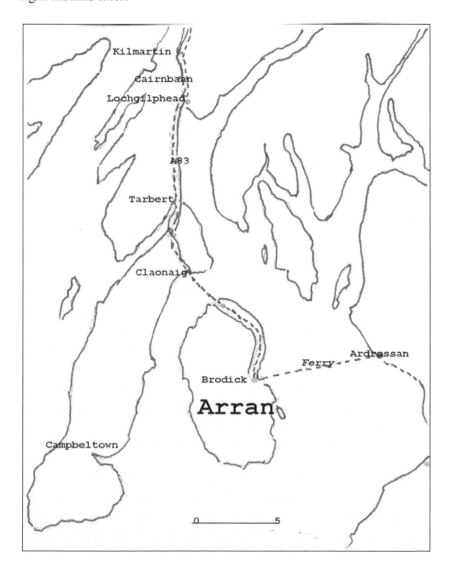

Ardrossan to Kilmartin: 16 May 1993

E ven though it was now the middle of May, a fresh fall of snow whitened the hills as I cycled onto the early-morning ferry. The Caledonian MacBrayne boat was busy as usual, its day-trippers planning the order of their ferry activities for the fifty-five minute crossing to Arran. It would be a busy schedule, a typical trip including one hot or cold beverage, a minimum of two photographs, several attempts at walking round the deck – 'My God, it's cold out there' – and at least one stumble across the raised entrance to the toilets. There wasn't enough time to listen to all of those safety announcements coming across the Tannoy: just enough to be puzzled about the meaning and whereabouts of the nearest muster point. Muster sounds a very chummy word to describe a gathering point although the wordless Euro signs of arrows pointing in all directions conveyed a greater sense of panic. I joined one of the queues at the ticket office to take my mind off the anxieties of mustering.

There were many cyclists on board, all of them looking ferociously fit and healthy. Just the sight of them brought on a twinge in my right knee. I retired to the top deck to find somewhere quiet to rub ointment into my worried joint. I found an empty area on the top deck where, as soon as I began to expose my lower leg, crowds began to gather. I tried to look suitably nonchalant as I rolled down my trouser leg and limped off to the fore deck to loose off my quota of ferry photos. Despite the icy wind, I had to elbow and rucksack my way through to the front of a large group of hardy passengers – all lenses and 'Christ, it's cold out here'. As a misty Goat Fell only merits one, or at most two, snaps, some of the ferry photographers were keen to find something else to focus on. One man was twisting a lens at a coil of rope, a good one for the family film show: 'This is the majestic outline of Arran – Scotland in miniature – and this one is a coil of rope on the ferry.' 'That's nice, dear. Have you got any with people in them?'

As we neared Brodick, I made my way down to the car deck to join the other cyclists. It looked as if they all belonged to one large group, chatting eagerly as we waited for the cars, trucks, caravans and motorbikes to be waved through the bow doors of the ferry. We then swarmed up the gangway together, enjoying the simple pleasure of an island arrival; there is something special about cycling off a ferry. In the case of Arran, the landscape is noticeably different from the Ayrshire coast and Brodick in the sunshine has very much a bucket-and-spade holiday-look about it, confirming to visitors that they've escaped mainland duties.

Anxious to get away from the other pedallers, I was relieved to see that they were stopping at the shops. However, my pace was so slow that I hadn't even passed the golf course on the outskirts of Brodick before the 'chase' group whirred past me. Presumably they had all stopped to rc-group and it was not long before the whole peleton, all clicking gears and muscles, brushed me aside. Fortunately, they headed up the String Road that crosses to the other side of the island, leaving my ego and me the coast road north to ourselves. I had this fond belief that cycling must be helping me lose weight, but when fellow cyclists swept me off the road like that, I began to have my doubts. I was disappointed to read recently that whilst cycling at 12 mph is incredibly good for you if your heart is up to it, pedalling at 5 mph is no more strenuous than walking. At the pace I was travelling, I might actually have been gaining weight, particularly with so many feeding stops to avoid any risk of critical energy loss.

The A841, which circles the whole island, passes through woodlands shortly after leaving Brodick. The warm sunshine brought out the colour and smell of the trees. Bluebells and cream yellow primroses provided splashes in the hedgerows and all seemed well with the world. I stopped at Brodick's old quay where the road is steered down to the shore by the lower slopes of Goat Fell, and watched the ferry's distinctive red funnel make its way back across Brodick Bay. In the water, there was a group of seals bobbing up and then disappearing with playful (or was it sexual?) grunts. Holy Island, bought in 1991 as a spiritual retreat by Buddhist monks, rose up on the distant side of the bay. They clearly know a godly place when they see one. Was it just the name? Maybe Holy Loch could be available as a hallowed double now that the Americans have left their base.

The harbour at Corrie, Isle of Arran

The road northwards follows the shore for the next few miles and passes through the small village of Corrie, its row of white painted houses clustered round the small harbour. The bollards on the pier are in the shape of sheep, which, like the children's swings at the roadside, seem typical of Arran in its reluctance to take itself too seriously. However, my spring euphoria disappeared a couple of miles north of Corrie when the road leaves the flat route along the coast and heads inland at Sannox. For the next four miles, it climbed six hundred feet, taking me closer to the peaks of Arran's sharp-crested mountain range. The sun disappeared behind low cloud as I wearied my way up that road to reach the summit of the pass across the hills. About an hour from Corrie, I stopped for a rest at the top, partly to enjoy the view, but mainly to stop hyperventilating. Not only does Arran look like a fairy tale island, it also has some wonderful storybook names to describe its mountains. I looked across to the Peak of the Castles and the gaping gash in the rock ridge known as the Witch's Step. So who came up with the name of Goat Fell for the highest peak?

The road then plunges down Glen Chalmadale towards Lochranza. I clung on to my juddering brakes, covering the next four miles in about ten minutes. It is a beautiful glen, growing greener as it nears the sea, though I had little time to take my eyes off the road surface. Arran's most northerly village, Lochranza, was a good place to relax and enjoy a leisurely lunch. Whilst waiting for the next ferry crossing, I had a look round the castle fortress which guarded the sheltered bay.

Leaving the north of Arran

I was looking forward to making my first crossing on the ferry from Lochranza to Claonaig on the Mull of Kintyre, heading further west and back to the mainland. Caledonian MacBrayne use a smaller ferry on this short crossing and despite more icy winds, it was worth it for the views. A squall moved up the Kilbrannan sound, whipping up the waves as we made our way across, cameras clicking at the hills towering above Lochranza. Just as the ferries vary in size according to the different crossings, so do the landing piers and today they seemed to be getting smaller. I had started the day leaving the substantial port of Ardrossan and then landed at a reasonably large pier in Brodick. The boarding point at Lochranza was just a small slipway. Now, as we approached Claonaig, not even a ramp was visible. Perhaps we were going to make a landing on the beach? I must have seen too many of those 1950s' war films because I looked across to see if there was a duffle-coated Jack Hawkins on the bridge. Just as I became convinced that we were about to run aground, some rocks on the shore transformed into a small concrete slipway. The ferry's front ramp was lowered and we were soon on dry land again. 'That was a close one, Skipper'.

Caledonian MacBrayne ferry leaving Claonaig

Not only was there no harbour, there didn't seem to be a village at Claonaig. It was as if you had arrived at nowhere in particular. Even though the B8001 road down to the ferry definitely had a 'this can't be the right route' look about it, it does cross the northern tip of Kintyre and over to Kennacraig on West Loch Tarbert. I soon realised that I had another hill climb to negotiate as the road makes its way up onto the high windswept grasslands above Claonaig. The rain came on again, sweeping up from the south, forcing me into Berghaus blue for the first time on the trip. During all the zipping and unpacking of a lengthy waterproof wrapping, I looked back at the grey panorama of Arran's mountains. Later on, high up in the hills, I passed a solitary house where children played in the garden. Something about the age and size of the children suggested that it was a holiday home. I couldn't work out why they didn't look like locals. Perhaps it is because you don't run about laughing in the rain if you're at home. It's a serious business being a local – anywhere.

The rain had stopped by the time I descended into the gentle rolling countryside around Kennacraig on the other side of the peninsula. The hedges, fields and woodlands were in sharp contrast to the bleakness of the high moorland which I had just crossed. I was surprised to see the signpost for the Caledonian MacBrayne ferry to Islay, having for some reason always thought that this island was further north, nearer to Oban.

Kintyre hangs like a loose tooth from its northern neighbouring district of Knapdale, as the west and east lochs almost meet at Tarbert. I later discovered that the word 'Tarbert' means a narrow neck of land, which is why the name is so frequently used in the west of Scotland. Apparently it was common to 'sail' galleys across these necks of land, using tree trunks as rollers. Needless to say, Bruce, who occupied Tarbert castle for a time, used the roller coaster technique and before him, King Magnus Barefoot in 1093. The fishing port of Tarbert was grander than I had expected, tucked away in a snug dip in the hills. The tide was out and the mud was in. Even so, the curving harbour promenade looked impressive. The tall church tower and Tarbert Castle add to the self-important air of what was once a busy and prosperous fishing port and there is still a ferry link eastwards across Loch Fyne to Portavadie on the Cowal peninsula.

The town, nevertheless, had that suspended Sunday-afternoon feeling about it.

Thirty miles of pedalling was beginning to tire me as I cycled up the hill out of Tarbert and across the wooded headland. I was travelling as light as possible, using a medium-sized rucksack strapped to the rear carrier frame. I knew that I would have to carry the bicycle for short sections of the journey and there was no way that I could lift a bike laden with paniers. I won't embarrass myself by revealing just how few changes of clothes I carried. Inevitably, when the rucksack had to contain essential equipment: waterproofs; a fleecy jacket; lightweight shoes; sheet sleeping bag for staying in hostels; maps; a camera; a walkman and tapes, there was little room for 'spares'. The rest of the space was taken up with the minimum of toiletries and a range of medicinal creams.

Small though the baggage might have been, it was a relief to find that the road soon dropped back down to the shores of Loch Fyne and remained level, close to the water's edge, all the way to Lochgilphead. Looking back down the loch, I could still see the sharp outline of the snow-clad peaks of Arran. I thought about stopping in Ardrishaig and finding somewhere to stay in one of its neat houses with decorative gardens, all azaleas and freshly-cut lawns. It was best, however, to keep going whilst the weather was so good.

I by-passed Lochgilphead and then picked up a little, very little, speed as I cycled alongside the Crinan Canal. I had a look at the lock gates at Cairnbaan where the canal reaches its highest point as it cuts through the neck of the Knapdale and Kintyre peninsula. Disappointed that I couldn't see any B&B signs, there was little option but to continue cycling northwards along the A816 towards Kilmartin.

Over forty hilly miles had changed unfit legs into weary ones aching for a rest. It was some consolation that the last few miles to Kilmartin were through the flat open countryside of the Mòine Mhòr. It had been a day for discovering great names: first King Magnus Barefoot and now a place he was presumably happy to walk on, The Great Moss. This part of the country, known as the cradle of Scotland, is littered with the archaeological crumbs of past civilisations and the flatness of the landscape contributes to the eerie and almost mystical atmosphere. Everywhere I looked, there seemed to be solemn standing stones and chambered cairns and, at Templewood, a stone circle stood brooding in a copse of oak trees and ancient monument signs.

From here the road rises steadily to reach the village of Kilmartin, set high up on a ridge overlooking the plateau of the great moss. By now I was so exhausted that when I finally did find Mrs McAuslan's B&B sign, I could barely talk. It took me three attempts to ask if she had a room. Much to my relief, she was not put off by the jabbering of a bedraggled pedaller and showed me up to the small room which she 'kept for the singles'. I asked her if I could take a shower 'because I wanted a bath' and she explained that she didn't have a shower. But I could have a bath. I gave up trying to talk sensibly and limped upstairs to the comfort of her large old-fashioned bathroom to peel off clothes. It was big enough for an echo across the tiled floor and it was a place to spend time in. It felt so good to be there. Slowly the tiredness eased out of me to be replaced, in my hierarchy of needs, by the overwhelming desire for a pint.

I crossed to the churchyard on my way to the pub to look at the ancient Celtic crosses. The low evening sunlight shone across the green lands of the great moss as it had done for the centuries since these stones were carved with timeless designs. As the hotel was more recent and didn't look too inviting, I settled for a pint of fizzy beer in the bar of a local restaurant instead. The staff must have undergone some fierce customer-care training programme and insisted that I took a seat to spare me the onerous burden of carrying my drink from the bar to a table. 'Would sir care to order now?' Clearly, at 7.40, it was already far too late to be ordering a bar meal. I declined and savoured the delights of a ghastly Highland pint for five minutes before the bar meals' menu was brought across to the table. After a few more sips and frequent glances from the barman, I gave up all hope of having a drink in peace and ordered the 'Fresh Loch Fyne Haddock'. I asked whether there were any haddock left in Loch Fyne. 'Chips or boiled?' came the witty riposte. The fish tasted good but the service was unrelenting and every time I put down my knife and fork, a head looked round the door to see if I had finished. By five past eight, I was out on the street again among the other tourists, facing a long evening ahead, and wondering why people who choose to eat bar meals have to eat up and be gone before the grown-ups arrive for dinner in the restaurant.

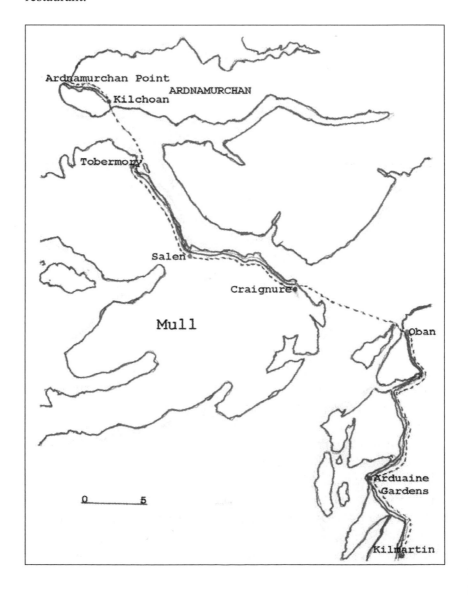

Kilmartin to Oban

Most people, I suspect, take breakfast in silence, gently easing themselves into the day. Hotels allow guests to retain a respectable measure of unsociability but look up from your cornflakes at the wrong moment in your B&B and you're spinning out of conversational control. Before you know it, you have locked eye contact with 'I thought we might just drive down to Loch Lomond and lunch at that nice milk bar. Have you got any plans? Oban? Well that'll be nice. Just a pity about the rain! We were there last Tuesday, or was it Wednesday Gerald? This is our second week – you wouldn't believe it could be so hot and the views were just out of this world – and now all this rain just when you arrived. Such a shame! Are you staying long? Well, it's been nice talking to you. Hope the weather improves for the rest of your holiday.'

Mrs McAuslan clearly doubted the sense in cycling to Oban in the rain, and wondered why I wasn't at least raising money for charity. I shared her doubts about the weather as the mist was below the level of the tarmac and gushing streams flowed down both sides of the road. It was the kind of weather when a visit to the local graveyard could be the highlight of the day. In fact, a small queue of people had formed at the gates of Kilmartin churchyard waiting to look at the Celtic crosses inside the church. Carved in medieval times on cold grey stone, the lines on these silent crosses have been smoothed by centuries of touching. Despite their age, the engraved patterns look like modern designs. The steady rain outside encouraged a closer study of these revered monuments and their ancient history.

It was still raining when I left Kilmartin to set off up the A816 switchback road to Oban. Progress was slow, sluggish pedalling interspersed with spells of even slower pushing, but the scenery alone made it worthwhile. From Kilmartin, the road climbs to over 500 feet before turning west and descending to the shores of Loch Craignish. Even in the rain, the crumbling coastline looks beautiful, rugged hills tumbling down to a sea sprinkled with islands of all shapes and sizes.

The rain also tumbled and I caught a sideways soaking from the spray of a passing transit van. It was time to find shelter and the Loch Melfort Hotel, 'The finest location on the west coast' (for rain?), was a welcome sight. A range-rovered lady, whom I took to be the owner, watched me find a place to leave the bike near the front entrance before announcing that I 'looked wet'. 'You'll be looking for the bar', she added, fearful that I might be presumptuous enough to drip my way into the hotel foyer and frighten the paying guests. The tradesman's bar had a log fire, a picture-window view across Loch Melfort and an expanse of empty tables and chairs to let me unwrap and dry out in style. The man behind the bar was friendly enough despite his merry quip about it 'not being the best day for a cycle' and I collected a carrier bag from him to add to my rucksack waterproofing. I must have spent nearly an hour relaxing, unwrapping and wrapping waterproofs and watching the steam rise from my socks. People who are seriously wet can get away with a lot.

By the time I left, I fully agreed with the 'finest location' claim on the signpost, particularly when I discovered that the hotel was just next door to the gardens of Arduaine. Even in the rain the azaleas, bluebells and giant rhododendrons glowed against a backdrop of eucalyptus and pine trees. I say 'even in the rain' but there again I can't remember seeing any of these National Trust gardens in the sunshine. From Threave to Inverewe, rhododendrons have always produced for me that pattering sound.

I had the garden to myself to stroll round its woodland terraces, enjoying a fix of horticultural sedative. In fact, I was feeling so laid back when I left, that a few miles further on, I stopped to try and spot a cuckoo which was calling in the oak trees at the roadside. It stopped mid 'cuck' and I waited for some time to find out whether it would resume its call with an 'oo' or a 'cuck'. It was good to be out here pondering the big issues in life, but as the bird refused to reveal its secret intention, I pedalled on.

From Loch Melfort, the narrow road climbs back into the hills again for the next seven miles and enters a wilder and rockier landscape as it crosses over the headland. The road became even narrower and I felt the breath of passing trucks on my right knee. A slightly battered coach rolled towards me, the driver seemingly confident about travelling at such a speed so close to the edge of the road. He probably only felt a gentle sway as he passed the Dormobile van coming up behind me, perhaps even mildly surprised at the van driver's decision to polish his nearside wheels on the rocks at the side of the road. There was a grinding noise of metal meeting rock and then hubcaps spun past me like tops, rolling downhill along the road. Fortunately, only dignities were bruised and the coach driver drove off to cut another notch in his steering wheel. I took the descent down to Loch Feochan slightly more slowly, conscious of the relative structural properties of hubs and kneecaps.

There was a little 'leisure oasis' at Kilninver where the Scottish Salmon and Seafood Centre sheltered passing tourists from the rain. It was a pleasant enough place to have coffee – all pine, spotlights and herbal pastries – and I spent an easy half-hour watching glum-faced tourists empty out of their cars and coaches to enrich their knowledge of fish at this 'interpretive centre'. Perhaps their time spent in these creaking wicker chairs will have been the highlight of their rainy afternoon. There will have been just enough time to try on a scarf, buy a postcard and check the price of honey at the 'Loaves and Fishes' shop before returning to their rain-swept windscreens for the rest of the three-hour drive. I'm not sure why I was feeling so smug because all too soon I was waterproofing my way back out on the wet road to negotiate one of the many 'last hills' before Oban. Near Cleigh, one of the old red phone boxes had been felled and lay on its side looking surplus to requirement and rather forlorn even though the light was still on. The sight prompted a nod from me and a 'they don't make them like that anymore these days'. It looked like one of the old-fashioned 'Press Button A' phones which always make me think of Billy Connolly's story about the confused telephone operator talking to the drunk:

'Is there money in the box?'

'No I'm just here myself.'

Having finally pedalled up the last 'last' hill before Oban, I felt that I was entitled to a panoramic view of the town and surrounding area. Disappointment was in store for me when the road sidled in through the back streets. After so many miles of country roads, I was taken aback by the noise and speed of the traffic, and worse still, I had to negotiate roundabouts and decide on traffic lanes. By now, the rain had stopped and I could see where I was going and as often seems to happen in the late afternoon on the west coast, the sun finally decided to shine. The harbour was busy as usual, the red, white and black colours of the large ferries adding an air of importance and excitement to the town.

I made my way through the centre towards the Youth Hostel, one of a row of grand houses, now mostly hotels, on the seafront road to Ganavan. I had joined the Youth Hostel Association when I was about fifteen but had never set foot inside one till now. I had been frightened off by the regulated dormitory image. The notice on the front door stating the first two rules, or aids to communal living, before I had even entered the building, added to my years of doubt and trepidation. Once inside, my boots off, and the door firmly closed behind me, I was greeted by that claustrophobic smell of a hospital psychiatric ward – a combination of disinfectant and a hint of cooked cabbage. The warden took my card from me before I had a chance to escape and showed me round the large common rooms and my dormitory with six iron bunk beds. The kitchen was spacious enough with plenty of room to sit at leisure and count the currants in your backpackers' muesli. The lounge had chairs covered in non-destructive light-brown plastic upholstery and maybe it was just my imagination, but I'm sure that I saw one or two of the seated hostellers rocking gently. Perhaps I could still catch a boat to Mull tonight? But how could I get my card back from the warden? I had a quick and dangerous shower instead. When I couldn't find the light switch and rather than expose my hostelling innocence by asking someone, I closed the curtain and washed in darkness whilst attempting to keep my balance on a slippery sloping floor.

Having survived the shower, I felt much better and went into town for a drink. I felt better still following a couple of pints of reasonably decent beer in a seafront hotel and walked up to have a look at McCaig's Tower. This monumental folly, partly modelled on the Coliseum of Rome, was built by a local banker at the end of the last century to provide work to the unemployed. Set high on the hill at the back of the Victorian town, it provides a fine viewpoint across the Firth of Lorn.

Oban Harbour

I walked back down to the harbour to look at the high-mast sailing ship tied up at the north pier and watched the fishing boats unloading their catch. It was almost dark, and the lights guiding ships through the narrow channels out to the open sea were beginning to flash out their nightly messages before I reluctantly returned to the hostel.

In the dining area, some of the inmates were silently staring into their cups of hot chocolate while one or two were enjoying a bit of light rucksack re-packing. Having had enough excitement for one day, I retired to my dormitory. I instinctively knew that the man with the staring eyes, whom I had spotted earlier, would be waiting for me. Sure enough, there he was on the top bunk on the other side of the 'dorm'. I crept into bed, thankful that I was so tired that I fell asleep almost immediately – within the hour anyway. I must have been sleeping for well over five minutes before I awoke to his startled cries of 'Oh no, oh no', as he sat bolt upright in bed, creaking with anxiety. I pulled the pillow over my head, trying not to think about what he had just done or how he was going to clean it up.

The northern stretch of Oban from the Caledonian MacBrayne ferry

Oban to Kilchoan

I lay for what seemed like hours staring blankly at the ceiling rose, trying to work out whether Tuesday had started very early or Monday had never quite come to an end. At some point during a restless night, I must have dreamt that one of the lads turned up with two local girls, audibly surprised that the promised love nest was rather crowded! When too much daylight could no longer be ignored, I stumbled out of bed, silently cursing all around me. Downstairs, there was already some serious muesli munching in the canteen area and more rucksack packing in the hall. I retrieved my card from the warden and escaped into early-morning Oban.

The weather looked better than the previous day. A hint of sun appeared from behind the clouds as I cycled down the ramp of the Caledonian MacBrayne ferry for the forty-minute crossing to Craignure on Mull. Leaving the shelter of the sound of Kerrera, we felt the full force of the high winds blowing in from the Atlantic as we sailed out into the Firth of Lorn. Despite the weather, many of the passengers still gathered on the upper deck to catch a view of the 'congregation' of mountains whose peaks line the shores of Loch Linnhe to the east. The snow-covered mountains in the Ben Nevis range, together with the Glen Etive hills and Ben Cruachan, looked threatening in the stormy gloom.

The ferry was reassuringly stable despite the force of the wind that was battering the mountains of Morvern and blowing waterfalls back up the crags, forming showers of spray on the crest of the hills. Having left such a large and busy port as Oban, it was strange to be approaching the rather insignificant-looking pier head at Craignure. The castle at Duart Point, which guards the entrance to Craignure Bay, looked imposing, while the rest of Mull appeared to have turned its back on the mainland. I was glad to be cycling in the east of the island and sheltered from the strong wind that would have slowed me to a walking pace.

Several groups of seals were relaxing on the rocky shore alongside the flat A849 road north to Salen and up the side of the Sound of Mull. The sun came out and I felt good cycling this morning, enjoying the flatness and a following wind. It only took me forty-five minutes to cover the eleven miles to Salen: very good timing for me.

View south down the Sound of Mull

Signposted for miles, the small village of Salen is easily missed. Most roads on Mull seem to lead to it because the west coast of the island almost meets the east coast at this narrow neck of land. The village was founded by the 'father of Australia', Lachlan MacQuarie. Quite what fathering a country involves remains a mystery to me but it sounds like a job for someone with a name like Lachlan MacQuarrie.

The road to Tobermory climbs across gentle slopes overlooking the Sound of Mull. The fields were sprinkled with white flowers and the views, both up towards the Ardnamurchan peninsula and back down to the blue hills of the mainland, provided frequent reasons to stop and stare. To the south-west, the top of Ben More, the island's highest peak at 3171 feet, was still in mist while the rest of the gently rolling hills of the surrounding countryside looked relaxed in orchard green. There is a stark contrast here between the overwhelming dullness of the island in rain to the pervasive mulled tranquillity of sunshine when the island's tragic past, the loss of 85% of the population in the nineteenth century to make way for sheep, is easily forgotten.

The Sound of Mull north to Ardnamurchan

Tobermory is tucked away in a hollow in the hills, hidden from the main road until you're right on top of it. Then it is a steep descent down to the row of brightly painted houses lining the waterfront. There is an ocean-going feel about the place and it is not difficult to imagine the sunken wreck of the Spanish Armada galleon lying at the bottom of Tobermory Bay. When the Youth Hostel where I had planned to spend the night was closed till late afternoon, I wondered about crossing over to Ardnamurchan, the arm of the mainland stretching out over the north of Mull. The sight of the eye-staring hosteller from Oban increased my desire to leave. At the tourist office, there was some doubt about accommodation at Kilchoan in Ardnamurchan and anyway, the high winds could force Caledonian MacBrayne to cancel further crossings from Tobermory to Kilchoan for the day. It was strange how the plan to reach Ardnamurchan today, simply a vague thought an hour earlier, suddenly became so urgent. Was the tourist office over pessimistic, or was I likely to face a night under a hedge somewhere? When I returned an hour later, I was told that the ferry would make one last crossing despite the gales. I hurried down to the pier.

Even though Caledonian MacBrayne uses one of its smaller boats for the crossing to Kilchoan, there was no difficulty in finding a place for my bicycle on an empty car deck. As we left the pier, I realised that, not only was my bicycle the only vehicle, I was the sole passenger. How grand it felt to be cruising on my personal ferry! The ferry company's reputation rose even higher in my estimation, although I couldn't quite understand their caution about sailing out of the relatively calm waters of Tobermory Bay. However, as we crossed Bloody Bay on the north-east coast of the island to leave the Sound of Mull, the full force of the Atlantic storm winds hit us. For the next twenty minutes, the boat steadily ploughed its way through the high waves, crossing the entrance to wild Loch Sunart and into Kilchoan Bay on the rocky coastline of Ardnamurchan.

In good weather, the ferry docks at the Kilchoan slipway to allow the cars to be driven off. Today, the sea swell was too high to use the slipway and we would be docking briefly at the pier. The full effect of the wind became apparent when the captain turned the boat to bring it alongside the pier and we began to pitch and toss wildly. When the landing rope dropped short of the three waiting on the pier, the boat then turned back towards Mull. Just when I thought that the captain had given up, he turned again in a wider arc to bring the ferry even closer in. This time the rope was caught and the crew hastily pushed a narrow metal gangway across the gap between the tossing boat and the pier. I hurriedly carried the bike across and reached the safety of the pier head. By the time I looked back, the gangway had been pulled in and the ferry was heading back out across the Sound of Mull to the safer waters of Tobermory Bay. What might have been a routine event for the ferry crew was for me an exciting way to arrive, for the first time, in this distant part of the Scottish mainland.

Thanks to the lady in the tourist caravan, there would be no difficulty in finding accommodation. One place couldn't be contacted because it was run by the local coastguard and he was out dealing with a coaster in trouble off the north coast of the peninsula near Ockle where I would be heading the next day. In fact, there was no real shortage of places and I was soon sitting by the bedroom window in Mrs MacMillan's elegant house in Kilchoan watching a rainstorm sweep across the Sound of Mull. The clouds then cleared and the sun began to shine on the north coast of Mull as I set off to cycle the five miles to Ardnamurchan Point.

From Kilchoan, the road, heading across rolling countryside sheltered from the Atlantic by the craggy coastal hills, offered, until I arrived at the Point, only a few tantalising glimpses of the sea-blue horizon. I spent an hour sitting on rocks near the lighthouse at the end of Ardnamurchan watching the storm clouds drag their curtain of rain over distant Coll and Tiree. What a view! What a goal-scoring sense of achievement at just being there! I tried to photograph the colours of bright yellow lichen on the greyish green rocks, the clusters of flowering sea pinks and a sea changing from silver to blue as the clouds opened and closed above. The finest view of all was northwards to the islands of Muck and Eigg and the mountains of Rum. It was my first sight of the islands that would dominate the seaward view for much of the next few days. I was reluctant to leave this magical place to cycle back to Kilchoan. I listened to Leonard Cohen feeling like the 'bird on the wire', or more likely the 'drunk in the midnight choir,' as I tried, in my own way, to feel free.

Kilchoan to Lochailort

The winds had died down overnight and the clouds were high as I left Kilchoan next morning, heading eastwards along the narrow B8007. This is the only route into Ardnamurchan for the motorist. Its long, twisted miles along the southern coast of the peninsula keep much of the mainland traffic at a distance and create that sense of remoteness normally only found in the islands. Shortly after leaving Kilchoan, the road travels northwards around the slopes of the elegantly-shaped Ben Hiant and climbs for 400 feet to cross over the spine of the peninsula. Looking south across to Mull, the snow on the top of Ben More gave me an excuse to stop and rest early-morning legs. Just after the highest point, I took the side road to the left off the main road and began the descent down to the small village of Kilmory on the north coast of Ardnamurchan. From here I was hoping to cross over the hills on a track or path to reach Kentra Bay, near Acharacle, further up the coast.

Rum and Eigg from Ardnamurchan

I stopped again on the way down to Kilmory to look at the beautiful view of the sea and mountains. The closely-cropped grass of the sloping foreshore shone lime green in the bright morning sunshine, and at the water's edge, dark rocks were scattered along the sands. The colour of the sea changed from turquoise in the shallows to a darker blue, and in the distance there stood as fine an array of hills as you will see anywhere. The flattened shape of Eigg was close enough for me to pick out some of the island's houses and fields, and behind, the steep slopes of Sgurr nan Gillean on Rum rose up out of the sea. Further north, I could clearly make out the familiar shape of the Cuillin Ridge on Skye with Glen Sligachan separating the other Sgurr nan Gillean from the hills of Marsco and Blà Bheinn. Here already was a feast of magnificent mountains on the horizon; the mainland hills of Morar and Knoydart would follow later in the week.

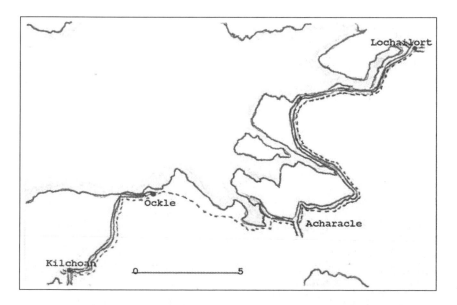

The road eastwards from Kilmory had been recently resurfaced and it was good to cycle on new tarmac for the next few miles along the coast to the small group of houses at Ockle. From here, I took the stony track that climbs steeply up the hill behind the village. It was hard work gaining height and, with a darkening sky, I began to think more and more about the next nine miles over the hills, wondering whether I could cross them with the bike. There were several gates to negotiate on the way up from the village and at the third one, near the top of the ridge, I found a sheep lying across the track. It looked as if it had got its head caught under the bottom rail of the gate. If I opened the metal gate carefully, I might be able to free it. 'I'll soon get you out of there,' I said confidently in my best animal gate-side manner and looked encouragingly into the sheep's eyes. The sheep seemed unimpressed by this show of veterinary skills and stared back at me impassively. Admittedly, I can't claim to be an expert on sheep, having once asked some Yorkshire farmers whether they were rearing Pentlands for wool or meat. Why should I have heard of Pentland potatoes? Confident that I could at least tell one end of a sheep from the other, it came as something of a surprise when, as I slowly opened the gate, the sheep rolled over to reveal that the other end also had a head on it. This one had horns and seemed to display more signs of life than the one that I had just been trying to reassure. It took me a minute or two to deduce that either this sheep had a head at each end or it was in the process of giving birth to a lamb. Now I really did feel inadequate, my midwifery skills being even poorer than my farming ones. The first solution I came up with was to just carry on cycling and pretend that I hadn't noticed it. Needless to say, my better nature and another glance at the mother's front end quickly made me realise that I should attempt to get help. Or was it because I couldn't get the gate shut?

I walked back down the hill and told the first person I met in Ockle about my problem sheep. Thankfully, he agreed to come and have a look. As soon as he saw that the sheep was on its back he knew that there was something wrong. He succeeded in pulling the stillborn lamb part of the way out of the mother's womb but couldn't release it completely. Together we managed to heave the sheep onto its feet. Part of the problem had been that she hadn't been able to get off her back to assist with the delivery, or so I was told. It was a sad sight to see the sheep stagger across the path with a lamb trailing behind her.

Remarkably, within a couple of minutes, she had wandered across the heather and got her head down for some serious eating. We left her to it with promises to let the local shepherd know.

A little further on, the ground flattened out and I was able to cycle along the rough track for the next couple of miles. The only person I met turned out to be the local shepherd. He assured me that if the sheep were eating again, she would survive. In any case, he would check on her.

This is a wild coastline with numerous rocky headlands stretching out into the sea where it was easy to see why a ship could be wrecked on these shores. Although I looked long and hard, there was no sign of the trawler that had been in difficulties off Ockle Point in the gales of the previous day. The track narrowed to a path and turned inland, away from the coast, and seemed to be heading straight into the hills. I looked at my map only to find that the dotted line of the path disappeared at this point. A compass bearing was therefore necessary to reassure myself that I was heading for the narrow gap in the hills. My doubts about the route increased as the weather continued to deteriorate and it was getting quite dark and decidedly stormy. As there was no chance of cycling at this stage, I shouldered the rucksack and pushed that bike over rocks and through bog until I reached the top of the pass. I wondered what I was doing there in the middle of nowhere, dragging a bike at my side and waiting for the rain. Part of the reason became obvious when I finally reached the top of the pass and started down the four-hundred-foot descent on the other side of the hill. Now the bike was a definite asset as I crunched, swerved and crashed my way down the track. I stopped near Gortenfern to have some lunch and looked across to the singing white sands of Kentra Bay. At least I'm told the sands sing in the wind but sadly, I didn't get to hear them. I can, however, vouch for their striking colour shining out of the grey surroundings.

I was relieved that the difficult part of the day's journey now seemed to be over, although I hadn't bargained for getting lost in the forestry tracks that surround Kentra Bay and keep Acharacle hidden from view. The rain changed from a drizzle to a downpour in less time than it took me to decide whether to extract my waterproofs from the rucksack. So I was now lost, very wet and anxious to get to some food and warmth at Acharacle. I had spent a long time going round in circles, I suspect. Eventually, more by luck and persistence than navigational skills, I emerged from the forest at the southern tip of the bay.

My morale, already dampened somewhat from the high point at Kilmory, was further soaked when I added to my problems by making some daft decisions. Firstly, I took a side road that by-passed Acharacle and then, on reaching the main A861, headed northwards rather than cycle a mile back into the village. Not having checked the map properly to find out how far it was to the next shop or village, and even though I was desperate for something hot to drink and some warmth to dry out, I wasn't prepared to pedal that one mile back to Acharacle. It soon became clear that I had several cold, wet and very hilly miles to cover before reaching that hot cup of coffee and freshly-baked doughnut. My mind-set was that of a city car driver rather than a cyclist, utterly unaware that I was unlikely to come across many houses, let alone 'the drenched doughnut', for the next eighteen miles.

It never ceases to amaze me that, just when I think that I've come to the end of a series of bad decisions, I still have the capacity to make an even dafter one. So, for a reason that still mystifies me, I cycled past the only restaurant that I came across, near Kinlochmoidart, to head on for Glenuig because, apparently, it had a Post Office. I can only assume that rain water had now penetrated the brain – it had trickled into every other part of my body – because the sudden desire to use the postal services came as a bit of a surprise. Had it something to do with buying a stamp? Needless to say, the Post Office was long closed when I oozed my way into the tiny village at half-past-five in the evening. Despite the pouring rain, Glenuig looked to be a fine place, overlooking the Sound of Arisaig. Its hotel certainly seemed worth a visit. I left my bike in the porch and went inside to the small bar, aloud with laughter, wedding guests and pipers. Feeling very out of place, an intruder at someone else's party, dismal and waterlogged, I retreated back into the rain. There was little alternative but to keep on pedalling up the coast towards Lochailort.

The road along by the sea and shores of Loch Ailort is very beautiful. Across the bay, there were plenty of islands to catch the eye and imagination and at the roadside were lush avenues of rhododendrons and tall pine trees. But now, early evening, I just wanted to gaze at a B&B sign. Cold and tired, I was at my lowest point since the trip began. I even considered catching a train home the next day. The nine miles to Lochailort seemed to take forever. Although no distance in a car, the gap of eight to ten miles between the villages, when tired and knackered, meant a lot of pedalling. I just hoped that there was somewhere to stay in Lochailort because I didn't have the legs for another ten-mile stretch. I passed a large grey mansion near the village and watched as an elderly couple walked slowly across the gravel courtyard. A pack of hunting dogs met them at the front door like a scene in a film, all atmosphere, and gravel-crunching sound effects. I could feel the silence behind those tall black windows when they had disappeared inside.

The road to Lochailort

It is not the largest of places, Lochailort. Despite its size, it proudly lays claim to a West Highland Railway station and is an important junction where the road from Glenuig meets the Fort William to Mallaig 'Road to the isles'. Modest though its claim to fame might be, on this wet Wednesday, it seemed like a city centre, with not one, but two, B&Bs and a hotel to choose from. When the B&Bs along the Glenfinnan road were full, the hotel was my last hope and I must have looked a sorry sight as I waded into reception. I certainly felt a sight and the man who answered the reception bell looked me up and down carefully before somewhat grudgingly offering me a room. It was a small single room with wood-panelled walls, tucked away at the back of the hotel. No matter! It was so good to have somewhere out of the rain where I could peel off the layers of wet clothing. If you have ever been really soaked through, you will be familiar with the slow process of stripping off each soggy layer followed by that satisfying skin-tingling warmth which returns as the bath or shower water restores normal body temperature. Once dry and warm again, I went down to the bar and found a seat by the open log fire. The barman poured an impressively large glass of thick, dark oak-red wine. None of your feeble 'house red' here but a bulky Australian wine to restore some colour! The hotel served up steak pie and, after another slice of red wine, I dismissed all thoughts of catching any train tomorrow.

Collecting the wet clothes which the hotel owner had kindly dried out for me, I left the bar. I was cheered even more when I got outside to find that the rain clouds had dispersed and left behind a clear blue sky and warm evening sunshine. Yet again I realised that I had been caught out by the west-coast weather. It can rain all day with such a determination that you think it will never stop. Then you briefly turn your back on it, often in the early evening, and the sun returns as if it had never been away. The damp landscape had been transformed and I could now see the hills of Moidart across the calm waters of Loch Ailort.

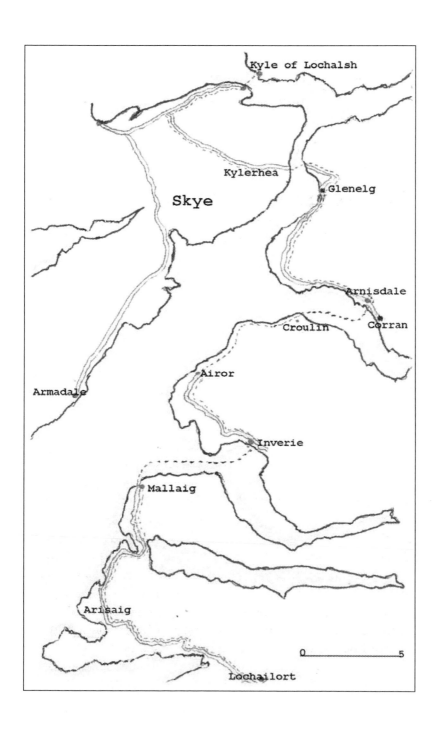

Lochailort to Inverie

There was one other resident down for breakfast, a regular, judging from his chatty banter with the hotel owner. He knew about the local area and its Churchillian and *Local Hero* connections. Churchill had been in the area to establish the headquarters of the Special Boat Service in the big house which I had passed yesterday. The residents' lounge of the Lochailort Hotel had been used as the dining room in the film *Local Hero* and after breakfast I went to see the wood-panelled room where the rescued rabbit was eaten for dinner. Even Burt Lancaster had been here: presumably not in the 'singles' room. Of interest also were other locations in the area which featured in the film, and the beach at Arisaig which was offered to the oil company for a fistful of sand.

Rum and Eigg from the beach near Arisaig

As the road westwards to Arisaig climbs slowly up from Lochailort, there are fine views to the south across the loch. When yesterday's tired legs were not as keen as the rest of me to get back on the road again, it really was a slow climb. I passed the *Local Hero* church standing aloof on the hillside, and then stopped to watch for trains on the West Highland railway line that follows the road at this point. A diesel train rolled lazily by but I was really hoping to see one of the steam trains travelling from Fort William to Mallaig.

It was a glorious day with hardly a cloud in the sky and the road, which threads its way through wooded glades, thick with rhododendrons, was as beautiful as I had been led to believe. The sunshine warmed the scent of the wild honeysuckle and azaleas sprinkled in the hedgerows. The views changed as the road dipped into dark forests and then opened up to the sea on the shores of Loch Nan Uamh where Bonnie Prince Charlie made his entrance and exit in 1745/6. I stopped at the Post Office in Arisaig and sat on one of the seats outside to write some cards and look across to Eigg and Rum.

There was another hill climb out of Arisaig to be negotiated on the main road northwards and then almost immediately a sharp descent to the sea again at the strangely named village, Back of Keppoch. For the next few miles, the road winds round the edge of small bays and coves, rarely straying far from the beach,. The woodlands on the Lochailort road cleared to expose flat open moor and grassland with views to the distant hills on Skye and, beyond Morar, to Knoydart. A strip of grey tarmac forms a thin dividing line between the beautiful white sands and the greenery of the machair. This is a fine route for cycling, past caravan sites and golf courses, where there is such a feeling of space that neither seems particularly intrusive. All you need to do is to walk over the sand dunes to find a near-deserted beach. Even so, I had to ask for help to find Peter's *Local Hero* beach which is hidden from the road. The curve of swept sand, edged by lichen-crusted rocks, made it easy to see why it had been chosen for a film location. Beyond the cream-coloured sands and blue waters, the sculpted outline of Rum completed an idyllic scene. I certainly wound through some celluloid, sensing that this had been my target destination all along. I was reluctant to leave and thought about staying at the Youth Hostel at Tràigh. However, as usual, the restless part of me won and I pressed on to see if I could find a way across to

Knoydart. Just the chance that I might see Knoydart in the sunshine for the first time was an incentive to continue.

I stopped again at the narrow estuary near Morar to look at the stretch of white silica sand at the edge of the blue green water. It is one of those places in Scotland, like the falls at Killin, where all but the most hard-bitten auto-tourist feels compelled to stop and wind down the car window. Into the shallow bay, the waters from the hidden Loch Morar tumble a mere thirty feet down to the sea. That's not perhaps that strange except that the loch holds the deepest waters in Britain with underwater chasms dropping to over one thousand feet. I resisted the temptation to cycle the few hundred yards inland to look at the loch for signs of the monstrous Morag, a distant cousin of the fabled creature at Loch Ness. The allure of the corrugated iron architecture of Mallaig was too strong for me.

The harbour at Mallaig

On this bright sunny afternoon, the town looked at its most cheerful even though the sheds at the centre add little charm. The sight of large storage tanks as you enter the town doesn't exactly endear you to Mallaig either, and on a grey wet day, the only good thing about the town can be turning at the roundabout.

Mallaig, that day, had lost that end-of-the-road feeling it usually had in store for me. I somehow had to get across to Knoydart. There would not be a ferry until the next day, Friday. The man in the tourist office knew little about cycling in Knoydart and wasn't over optimistic about my plan to cycle round its western shore. He suggested that I ring the Estate Office in Inverie to see if Spanish John was coming across. Although the name conjured up thoughts of a swarthy pirate and Enid Blyton books, I later discovered the name referred to the boat and not the owner and neither was crossing anyway. It was suggested that I try to speak to the owner of the pub in Inverie who was apparently in Mallaig to collect a delivery of beer. I found him down at the pier and he agreed to give me a lift if I helped load the barrels onto his boat. This seemed like a good deal to me.

Approaching Inverie, Knoydart

Having found a way to cross Loch Nevis to Inverie, I now had to phone the boat owner in Arnisdale to see if he would take me across Loch Hourn when I reached the north side of Knoydart a day earlier than planned. We also had to agree a precise meeting point. I knew that there was some form of track around the western tip of Knoydart although I wasn't sure how far it would take a bicycle. Whatever the difficulties, as Croulin Point was unlikely to host other cyclists at that moment, the boat owner should be able to spot me.

Back at the busy harbour, we waited for the beer to be served. For once, I was in no hurry and sat on the harbour wall watching the world go by. I met someone who had been in the bar at the Lochailort Hotel the previous night and we talked about how difficult it must have been, in centuries past, to travel in this part of Scotland. Apparently, the reason many villages are not more than eight to ten miles apart is that ten miles was the limit of a laden horse's trek across these mountain roads. I was now beginning to appreciate the importance of the sea routes in linking remote communities.

At five o'clock when the publican gave up waiting for the beer lorry, we set off in the 'Joanne Arden'. It was a great way to travel into Knoydart and the views in all directions were impressive. To the west were the Cuillin hills on Skye and on our right the fjord-like water of Loch Nevis carving its way deep into the mainland. My eye settled on that thin strip of white on the far shore tucked at the water's edge below the towering mountains of Knoydart. The houses looked so small, only growing to full size as we approached the pier. I could now see the soft underside of Knoydart, its guesthouse, pub and neatly painted cottages. There were a few sensible walkers sitting on the bench outside the pub catching the last warmth of the evening sun whilst enjoying a pre-midge pint and the view of Rum to the South West. I was tempted to join them but thought that I'd better look for the bunkhouse the tourist office had recommended. When I was eventually directed to a whitewashed barn, I went inside and surveyed the sad surroundings. At twelve pounds a night I was expecting a bunkhouse *de luxe* and began to compose the opening paragraph of my letter of complaint about exploiting hillwalkers. However, after checking the map and directions again, I realised that there was another bunkhouse up on the hillside, behind the village at Torrie Shieling, a significant improvement on the first with wall-to-wall carpets, a fitted kitchen and a smell of opulence rather than socks. It was almost embarrassingly comfortable with pine furniture, a fitted kitchen and the luxury of a shower.

On the way down the hill to the pub, I came across two red deer trapped by the walls on either side of the track. For a second or two, they stood their ground as I approached and, having expected them to turn and scatter, I felt quite menaced by their stillness and staring eyes. I also felt rather foolish and vulnerable sitting astride my bike. Then, with a clatter of hooves on stone and a startled leap over the wall, they disappeared into the undergrowth. There was barely a ripple on the surface of Loch Nevis as I cycled along the avenue of beech trees at the water's edge and heard the call of peacocks. Was this really one of the last great wildernesses?

Inverie to the Kyle of Lochalsh

A s usual, I was rather slow to get up and it was ten o'clock by the time I cycled back down the hill to the village. The weather had changed; there were grey overcast skies and the tops of the hills were hidden in mist, no doubt recovering from yesterday's exposure. Fortunately, there was little wind. The sea was calm and the high clouds didn't look as if they would be dumping rain, for the present anyway. This would be one of the most exposed and isolated parts of my west-coast journey and I would have been reluctant to try and make it to Croulin, on the north side of Knoydart, if the weather had been bad. I knew from past experience that the Arnisdale boat owner, Mr McTavish, would attempt the crossing to meet me even if the weather were poor. Yet, I was fully aware that there was a limit to how much wind his small boat could handle. If the weather broke, I could be stranded. It was only thirteen miles around the western coast of Knoydart and I had more than enough time, even at my slow speed, providing the tracks were good enough for cycling. If I had to carry the bike for long distances and the wind blew, I would be struggling.

The single-track road out of Inverie ran along the shore for a mile or so before heading north across the hills to the small crofting community of Airor. After a steep climb, I reached level ground high up on the hillside. The next few miles were easy cycling with sweeping views out to sea. Knoydart continued to surprise me; instead of the boulder-strewn track that I expected, I was cycling on the smooth surface of recently laid tarmac and I had those six miles of road to myself. The other surprise was that this was no desolate rocky wilderness, but a green-edged coast that had obviously supported several communities in the past. I read later in the *Statistical Account of Scotland* records that a population of a thousand people lived in Knoydart in the year 1793. Of these 150 were Protestant and there was one Protestant missionary. There were 850 Catholics, one Catholic priest and one surgeon. A total of 800 people migrated from the district of Knoydart from the year 1770 to 1793. Emigration was followed by famine and, a little over a hundred years ago, the forced eviction of the remaining inhabitants to create this 'wilderness'.

The road ended at Airor, a few houses clustered around a sheltered harbour, but a rough boulder-track continued from the north end of the village. I stopped at the top of a rise and looked down at Airor as the sun briefly came out. The track drops back down to the edge of a shingly beach, eventually fading out altogether, leaving only a faint line on the grassy foreshore. It was pleasant to be cycling on the soft grass, hearing the crackle of white sea-shells under the tyres. John Merrill, in his book describing a long distance walk round the coast of Britain felt 'very close to God' on the path from Airor to Croulin. Whilst I could understand how remote landscape might encourage such a feeling of intimacy, it was the evidence of man's works that made me feel uneasy as I passed by a broken chapel and many silent ruins.

Just before Inverguseran, the next deserted village, the track fords the river Guiserein. I stopped for lunch and tried to work out how I was going to cross the deep water. Whilst I was eating my crushed lunch, I heard and then saw a three-wheeled motorbike coming down Gleann na Guiserein. I watched its easy progress across the hill slopes before realising that it was heading straight towards me. I was fairly sure that the driver would be coming to tell me to clear off his land – farmers rarely approach hill walkers or mountain bikers for a chat. Happily, it turned out to be the local shepherd who was quite happy to talk about the area and the route ahead of me.

I had only about three miles to go and two hours before meeting Mr McTavish. This last bit, however, was likely to be the slowest of the day. Fording the river in bare feet made progress slow, the intense cold of the water only partly anaesthetising the pain of walking on jagged stones in the river-bed.

Cycling beyond Inverguseran was easy as I continued on the flat grassy track which followed the coastline for the next two miles, first northwards and then turning east at the entrance to Loch Hourn. As soon as I reached this dark loch, the scenery changed and the sky seemed to blacken as steep-sided mountains crowded the water's edge. The loch of hell (Hourn) has a forbidding air about it in contrast to the brightness of the loch of heaven (Nevis) at Knoydart's southern edge. The track ahead disappeared into wooded cliffs and the way forward looked barred by the rocky lower slopes of the Ladhar Bheinn group of hills. The shepherd had warned me that the route across the crags involved some scrambling up through the rocks and trees onto the top of a ridge at Rubha Camas an t-Salainn. It was only a climb of some two hundred feet or so but the effort of carrying the bike on my shoulder, as well as a rucksack, was enough to exhaust me in a matter of minutes. I had to use my hands to hold onto the rock on the steeper sections which meant that I could only lift the bike up a few feet at a time, pause for a rest, and then go back down to take up the rucksack. It took me a long time to cross that mile of ridge. Coming down the steep path on the other side was slightly easier, with the bike kicking and rattling at my side as I fought to keep hold of it. The sight of a house below me on the edge of a curving bay was most welcome. For months, whilst planning my route, Croulin had been a key name on the map, one of the most difficult places for me to reach, and it was, therefore, very satisfying to see that it really existed. Of several buildings, only the large house looked occupied and I was curious to know what it would be like to live in such a remote place. Clearly, the boat would be the main form of transport, but how often would the occupants be cut off during winter storms? Although tempted to call, I pedalled on for another few hundred yards to the rocky point of Rubha an Daraich, and sat down to wait, enjoying a heady mix of achievement and isolation.

Further progress eastwards, along the coast, would have been impossible, high cliffs putting an end to cycle riding or carrying. I looked over the still waters of Loch Hourn towards Arnisdale and watched the mist moving across the slopes of Beinn Sgritheall on the far side. All the colours you could wish for were there today – so long as you liked grey.

For all my enjoyment of the peaceful setting, I was glad to hear the puttering sound of an outboard motor and see Mr McTavish's boat rounding the point. I had met him a couple of years previously when he had taken a group of us across to Barrisdale and, despite a storm blowing up in the late afternoon, he had kindly come to collect us. It was good to meet him again and enjoy his relaxed well-weighted humour on the short crossing to Arnisdale, and happily, there was room for the bike on his small, twelve-foot open boat. He proudly showed me the new baling pump which had replaced the saucepan since my last trip. When he pointed out some porpoises swimming alongside the boat, I could just see their backs curving in and out of the water.

Crossing Loch Hourn to Arnisdale. Mist on Beinn Sgritheall

In all too short a time, we had crossed those blackish waters and drifted silently into the bay at Arnisdale. Here the houses look as if they have been pushed into the waters of the loch by the slopes of Beinn Sgritheall towering above them. After Knoydart, this isolated village seemed almost urban by comparison, with cars on the road and even a rumour that there was a tea-shop in Corran, the cluster of houses at the very end of the road. The road to Glenelg, some eleven miles away, climbs steeply out of Arnisdale to cross the headland before dropping back down to the shore at Rarsaidh. There is a cluster of tiny islands close to the shore and fine views across the loch before the road enters the forest plantations. From here on, the tall pines only allowed occasional glimpses of Knoydart to relieve the seemingly endless climb round the south-western tip of the Glenelg peninsula. In fact, I was only about three miles from Glenelg village when the upward sloping tarmac finally relented and I descended the 500 feet down to Eilanreach in a matter of minutes. After a brief detour inland, the road remains close to the shore for the remaining mile to the quiet village of Glenelg.

Glenelg

The tourist brochure proclaims Glenelg as yet another 'hidden corner' of Scotland and it certainly retains a sense of remoteness despite not being short of visitors in years past. The Vikings came and chased the resident Picts into the safety of their Broch towers which can still be seen today. One broch is somewhat appropriately named Dun Troddan. Much later on, the English came and built barracks and Doctor Johnson nearly fell off his donkey crossing the high pass of

Mam Ratagan to get here. Doctor Johnson was clearly not impressed by the inn at Glenelg: 'Of the provisions the negative catalogue was very copious. Here were no meat, no milk, no bread, no eggs, no wine. We did not express much satisfaction. Here, however we were to stay. Whisky we might have, and I believe at last they caught a fowl and killed it.'[1] By contrast, my cup of coffee was OK. More recently, Gavin Maxwell came to write his book on otters, *Ring of Bright Water,* at nearby Sandaig.

Whilst I was in the hotel, the heavy shower of rain that had passed over the village left the air outside damp with the smell of the sea and hedgerow plants.

The main street of the unspoilt village is set back from the sea, sheltered amongst tall trees which form a grand avenue leading to the main road junction in Glenelg. When planning my route, the crossroads here had provided me with a dilemma. The road going east would take me over the high pass of Bealach Ratagan, to the magnificent views across Loch Duich to the Five Sisters of Kintail. It was from that route that Doctor Johnson entered Glenelg, but I turned left instead and made my way round the coast, past the castle barracks, to reach the ferry to Skye at Kylerhea. The Kyle is barely 500 yards across at this point, making for a strong tidal race at certain times of the day. A few years ago, there was some difficulty in finding someone to skipper the ferry and for a time it looked as if it might close. Sadly, the new bridge to Skye might put an end to this five-minute ferry crossing linking up some impressively wild country often ignored by motorists taking the fast route to the Kyle of Lochalsh.

I began to steel myself for a long climb up the Kylerhea glen to Bealach Udal, over 900 feet above me, every pedal of them from sea level. If I had been on my own, I would probably have walked up quite a bit of the hill but because of another cyclist from the ferry, the spirit of competitive companionship meant that I stayed in that saddle until every muscle in my body creaked to a standstill. 'Don't stop for me', she said, when I finally crumpled on the last steep bit of the ascent. Well, she was a lot younger than I was! I suspect she wasn't

[1] Samuel Johnson, *A Journey to the Western Island of Scotland.* Chapman & Dodd 1924

carrying such a heavy load either nor had she just crossed Knoydart –
not that I'm macho about these things! Never had I climbed a hill as
fast as I climbed that one! She even went down the hill faster than I
dared with a 'You go on ahead if you want to go faster'. I was
screwing all my courage to the handlebar just to keep up with her
startling descent. Despite it being good to have company, my ego was
relieved to part with her at the junction of the main road to Broadford.
She was turning left to flash off somewhere, probably Glasgow by
nightfall, and I went right, chain between my legs, to ache my way to
the end of this part of the journey at the Kyle of Lochalsh.

It was now early evening and the light drizzle looked as if it
would soon turn to some serious Skye rain as I headed for Kyleakin
and the ferry back to the mainland. The road crosses low-lying moors
and is not as dramatic an entrance to Skye as the route from Glenelg.
However, the ferry crossing, free to cyclists and pedestrians, always
generates some excitement. The same can't be said to be true of the
Kyle of Lochalsh which looked particularly gloomy on this grey
Saturday evening. I felt weary and sad that the week's cycling was
over. When the town's chip shops and privatised loo failed to
encourage me to stay, I turned and crossed back to Skye to stay the
night in Broadford and catch a glimpse of the hills.

The Broadford Youth Hostel was busy and after a quick
shower I retreated to the local hotel. As the bar was dark and noisy, I
took a seat in the large reception area, a typically luxurious feature of
many traditional Highland hotels: an initial impression of grandeur
until you see that your bedroom could fit into the fireplace in the hall.

The next day, I left the hostel at six, cycling out into a
glorious morning, the hills of the Red Cuillin glowing in the low
sunlight. I was already looking forward to continuing my journey the
following year from the Kyle of Lochalsh to Cape Wrath. I cycled
south towards Armadale and the first ferry of the day. There were very
few people about at this early hour and I was surprised to see a group
of what I took to be campers standing at the edge of a loch in the
middle of the open moorland. As I came nearer, I saw that they were
taking photographs of a man who stood motionless at the far side of

the water. He had his back to the hills and was dressed immaculately in flannels and jacket with creases that cut the early morning air – more lifestyle images for a glossy magazine of 'what young blades are wearing in the Highlands of Scotland this year', no doubt. I used up the remainder of my film on the ferry crossing to Mallaig, clicking at the mountains of Knoydart across the Sound of Sleat and nearly getting a picture of a group of dolphins as they leapt clear of the water.

Skye from the Kyle of Lochalsh

Kyle of Lochalsh to Kishorn: 14 May 1994

On any long journey, even the fittest of travellers will have some rest days. Taking a year out, however, might be considered somewhat excessive. I had returned home to Edinburgh the previous May, travelling by train along the West Highland line from Mallaig to Fort William. I rejoined my cycling route by taking another beautiful rail journey along the Highland line from Inverness to the Kyle of Lochalsh. There is a certain excitement about these railway journeys although it is difficult to book months ahead for one of two bicycle places and you often have to wait until other passengers have 'boarded' before the guard can tell you where to put the bike. Do we still 'board' trains?

In marked contrast to my last visit, the Kyle of Lochalsh was looking bright and cheerful, even though the view across to Skye was spoilt by what appeared to be mini oil rigs. But these 'oil rigs' would not be moving. They were the supports for a new bridge which would transform the area. No doubt, I would be back to gaze at the empty ferry slipway and reminisce about the old days when over the sea to Skye really meant something: often a long wait in summer.

Having rested for a year, it was hard work pedalling again and progress was slow along the beautiful coast road northwards to Erbusaig and Plockton. Both the road and railway keep close to the water's edge and I stopped frequently to enjoy the views across the Sound of Sleat to the snow-capped Cuillin hills on Skye. Small wonder that on the landward side of the road, there is a ribbon row of smart new houses with wall-to-wall panoramic windows and names like 'The Nest' and 'Odysey' (one 's' will do when you've got a view like ours!)

I followed the road inland to Drumbuie and then turned left to make my way down to the small village of Plockton tucked away in a forested cove. Plockton has everything you could ever want to look at on a Scottish calendar: a much-photographed huddle of houses, a row of 'look at those palm trees' along the sea front; an 'off-the-rails' restaurant and, surprisingly, its own airport. Presumably, if you can afford to live in Plockton, and there are a couple of 'Rollers' about to provide evidence of wealth, it is handy to have a place to land the old kite. The narrow main street was clogged up with four-wheel drive jeeps and hordes of day-trippers pouring out of road-width coaches. The sound of white heather music blared out of a radio on the beach

and I wanted to move on, slightly disappointed; Plockton had been more appealing in the rain when I had been here last.

Plockton

I cycled back up the hill out of the village, across the railway bridge, and turned left to follow a minor road through the forest to Achmore. There were only brief glimpses of Plockton Bay and a lot of uphill pedalling before the road emerged from the trees out onto the headland overlooking Stromeferry. Now I could see across Loch Carron to the sand-red cliffs of the Applecross hills and 'over the sea to Skye'.

I joined the main Lochalsh to Achnasheen road just after Achmore where some gate-leaning villagers smiled encouragingly at the sight of me toiling up the hill. Although it was getting very hot, their nods of support shamed me into waiting until I was hidden from their gaze before stopping for a rest.

I lost some hard-gained height on the steep descent towards Stromeferry, the ferry-less village, before climbing again to the next viewpoint. I still wasn't very sure where I would be able to stay and hadn't even decided whether to cross to Applecross the following day or take the more direct route to Shieldaig. My attempts at getting a boat from the Kyle of Lochalsh to Toscaig on the Applecross peninsula, or to find a boat owner to cross the loch at Stromeferry had been unsuccessful. The sight of spectacular hills on the other side of Loch Carron made me consider again the possibility of visiting the Applecross peninsula.

A combination of music on the walkman and the views up to the head of the loch eased some of the pain of the long ascent. At the summit, I stopped to breathe in the view of those formidable hills and, far below me, the waters of the loch flooding inland to Strathcarron, some eight miles away. The next two miles down to the shore sped by in an air-rushing, head-down descent. A hitchhiker, hearing my approach, but not bothering to look round, stuck his hand out and must have been surprised that the whispering Mercedes turned out to be a blob on a bicycle.

I was now more conscious of heading into the north-easterly breeze which was keeping the skies clear and the sun shining while weighing down the pedals. It was a long eight miles and there was another steep hill to climb before finally reaching the flat plain at Strathcarron. At last, I was able to turn out of the wind and head westwards again, back along the shore towards the village of Lochcarron. This side of the loch was sheltered by the circle of surrounding hills and a very lush-looking golf course running along the shore. A couple of hundred yards ahead of me, what appeared to be a highly skilled golfer drove his ball down the side of the fairway. Only a player with skill and a steely nerve would dare to aim so close to the road and that passing cyclist. Either that, I thought as I saw the white ball cutting through the air towards me, or he too had a 'hit and hope' game plan. When the ball hit the road a few yards in front of me and skimmed over my head to land in the ditch on the other side of the road, I decided on the latter. The statistical chances of being hit by a golf ball in this part of Scotland must be beyond most actuarial predictions, and certainly outside my policy cover.

I asked at the Lochcarron tourist office about getting some overnight accommodation in Applecross, nearly twenty miles and two and a half thousand feet away. It was a daft idea, but I was keen to move on a little further. Fortunately, although I didn't believe so at the time, guests at a wedding in Applecross had taken all available beds. Kishorn was suggested instead. While the prospect of spending the evening in a village with no hotel and staring at an oil rig did not enthral me, it would, nevertheless, make the next day's journey shorter. I set off up the hill at the back of the village, my legs weary as I made my way over the high road to Kishorn. Soon, regret at leaving the shores of Loch Carron set in. Not surprisingly, I was unprepared for the spectacular setting of Kishorn on the southern shore of the loch as the road curves round the bay to Achintraid. The small community at the water's edge, has an inspiring view across the loch to the towering cliffs of Applecross. When I booked in to the 'Craigellachie', a luxurious B&B in the centre of the village, it was difficult to stay indoors on such a warm sunny evening. A short rest, and I was off cycling back along the bay to look around. I had expected Kishorn Bay to be full of oil platforms but the only remains of the rig-building yard was an aimless looking pier on the far side of the loch. All that could be seen in the west that evening was the sun and, where Loch Kishorn escapes to the open sea, the Cuillin hills on a distant Skye and an even more distant Rum. I wasn't complaining.

View from Loch Kishorn to Skye

Kishorn to Torridon

There was porridge and conversation for breakfast which was a pity because I like porridge. Just one table was set for guests; it was at the window and, fortunately, a helicopter flew up and down the loch to disrupt our verbal stumblings. The owner explained that the metal canister, swinging like a pendulous milk churn beneath the helicopter, contained baby salmon lifted from the breeding grounds just up the glen. We watched as it was slowly lowered into a waiting boat moored in the loch. From here the salmon were taken out to one of the fish farms on the west coast. It was strange to see aerial ferrying of fish.

Our window view also revealed that the weather was still fine and Bealach na Ba, the pass across to Applecross, looked even higher this morning. This gave even more reason to mend a broken toe strap on the bike before leaving for the forty-seven miles to Torridon by the Applecross road. But those cliffs looked too enticing to pass by.

The wind was still blowing from the North East as I left Kishorn and it was hard going pedalling into it for the first few miles. It was a relief, albeit short-lived, to turn westwards off the main road and have the wind on my back as I started the two-thousand-foot climb up to Bealach na Ba, the 'Pass of the Cattle', to Applecross. Until recently, this was the only road into the peninsula, discouraging all but the most determined tourist. I had plenty of time to ponder on the name 'Applecross' which sounds as if it should be on the road between Oxford and Gloucester rather than in this wild country. There are several explanations for the origin of the name ranging from a planting of apple trees to the more likely corruption of a similar sounding Gaelic name. Not that I cared too much either way as I felt the full weight of the ascent in the pedals.

The lower slopes are on a relatively gentle incline and gain only a couple of hundred feet in the first mile, but as the road turns across the face of the mountain, Sgurr a' Chaorachain, it twists and climbs relentlessly upwards. I got off and pushed for a bit to give me more time to admire the view and rest from the pressure from the pedals. Further up the road, there were some other people pushing. Because they were behind a car trying to achieve a U-turn on the narrow road, it looked as if they were making an ignominious retreat back down the hill and I quickly remounted to enjoy the full smugness of the moment. As I passed, one of them confirmed that 'It's quicker by bike' as the ailing car cough-started its way back down to Kishorn.

Bealach na Ba, Applecross

There were wide open views down Loch Kishorn and over to Lochalsh and Glenelg, as slowly, very slowly, I pedalled uphill and into the shadows of the corrie formed by the cliffs of Meall Gorm. Despite the impressive dark surroundings, I still needed some music on the walkman. I mused on which pieces I would include in my eight Desert Island Discs. Roy Plumley has a lot to answer for. Some of us can spend a lifetime juggling those choices and neither Roy nor Sue ever thinks to ask for our final selection. My worst fear is being between lists and then being asked, at short notice, to fill in for an ailing Mick Jagger. I would have to spend a frantic weekend weighing up the merits of Gene Vincent's 'Be-bop-a-lu-la' and Berlioz's 'Te

Deum'. Sue Lawley made that phone call to the walker and artist Wainwright who had 'never cared for music very much' and chose, as a reminder of the hills, 'The Happy Wanderer' to prove it. Sue asked him how his wife felt about him walking on the Lakeland Fells all day and writing up his notes each night. 'It was an obsession, and it ended finally with my wife walking out and taking the dog, and I never saw her again'.

'And did you blame her?' asked Sue.

'Not at all,' Wainwright replied cheerfully. 'I don't know how she stuck it for thirty odd years. Right, what's your next question?'

I'm still waiting to be asked my first question but, despite all my years of patient short-listing, the phone has yet to ring.

At last I reached the back of the corrie where the road folds into a series of sharp hairpin bends that zig-zag their way up the steepest section of the pass. I had feared that this would be the toughest part but I managed to keep pedalling for those last few hundred yards by using the lowest gears on the bike and the highest level of endomorphins in my body. I was puffed-up with exhaustion and not a little pride as I reached the rock-strewn summit. Looking back down, the corrie cliffs framed the loch far below. To the west, Skye was stretched out in all its glory from the northern sea cliffs down to the snow-crested outline of the black Cuillin in the south. I also had my first clear sight of the Outer Isles, the last island companions on my journey up the west coast.

I eventually had to leave the barren rock plateau to find some shelter from the chill of the wind. The journey down was excitingly brief, especially when crosswinds blew me across the road and nearly over the edge of the hillside. It took me one and a half hours to climb to that Bealach and only twenty brake-shuddering minutes to hurtle down to sea level again. I had little time to adjust from the harsh mountain landscape to the gentle pastoral setting of the village of Applecross. It's not difficult to understand why a translation of the old name of this peninsula is 'sanctuary'.

After relaxing in the warm sunshine for a couple of hours, I left by the 'new' road heading round the north coast of the peninsula.

It seemed somehow incongruous to spot a sign just outside the village declaring that in 1976 Princess Margaret had opened the road connecting Applecross with Shieldaig. It has been built close to the coast and on this sharp-focused day, the blue contours of Skye and Raasay dominated views across the Sound. I stopped several times to enjoy the lonely setting and rest from the north-east wind. There are no houses or buildings to accompany this stretch of tarmac as it unravels along the coastline: just sea, islands and mountains. In fact, I couldn't see any sign of dwellings until, in the middle of nowhere, there was a 'School House'. A short distance later, I saw a group of stone-built crofts with corrugated iron roofs which looked as if they were now used as shelters for animals. The longer I looked at the deserted village of Kalnakill, the more traces of houses could be seen, some little more than piles of stones in the flat grassland. There must have been about twenty such ruins, perhaps housing a hundred people or more before the Clearances, part of the population of three thousand in Applecross in the middle of the last century.

I pressed on into the wind, tiring as the road crossed hillier ground. I was now walking up the steeper inclines, hoping that each rise would reveal the north coast of the peninsula. I passed a parked car as I plodded up one of those many hills and watched in fascination as a hand rose slowly and silently through the open sunroof clutching a segment of peeled orange. It took me a moment to realise that this act of wordless generosity was aimed at me. It was the best orange I've ever tasted.

Of the many great views on the west coast, few can match the one across Loch Torridon from the small crofting settlement at Fearnmore. The southern shore has been shattered into tiny coves with views over the loch to the wrinkled crags at Diabaig. I stopped to stare at the real centrepiece, the high peaks of Torridon, towering above the head of the loch, remembering days spent with friends on their high ridges, crossing the rock pinnacles of Liathach or scrambling over the horns of Beinn Alligin. I also needed time to gather up sufficient energy for the next eight or ten switchback miles to Shieldaig. The constantly changing view from the narrow road as it weaves in and out of the twisted coastline was about the only thing that kept me going: that, and the need to make a decision about what to eat and drink when I reached Shieldaig.

Loch Torridon

The road climbs high onto the hillside and then descends to the loch shore only to climb again, up through woodlands and crags and, from the brow, swoop down again, and again. I later found out that there were over two thousand feet of ascent on this short stretch of the road. Adding this to the earlier climb to Bealach na Ba meant a day's total equivalent to the height of Ben Nevis. No wonder I was becoming pre-occupied with eating. One of Samuel Beckett's characters, Murphy, spends a long time contemplating in which order to eat three assorted biscuits. Having decided to eat the two plain ones first and leave his favourite ginger biscuit to last, he lays them out on the grass. Whilst he is half way through the second one and looking forward to the best one, a dog comes along and devours the ginger biscuit. Such grief! Having at last settled on a pork pie washed down with a glass of ice-cold coke, I reached the village at five past five on this Sunday evening to find Shieldaig shut – Murphy's law. The hotel and shop were closed for tea, coke, peanuts, chocolate, rolls, and there wasn't even a glimpse of a doughnut through the closed net curtains. So it was back onto the main road, heading eastwards towards the next village of Torridon, some eight miles away. The road was now flatter and drier and the hills seemed to glow in the late afternoon sunlight streaming up the loch. Although it was exhilarating to be in the presence of these immense hills, tiredness drove me to the Youth Hostel, too exhausted to worry about all the 'No' signs at the doorway.

Loch Torridon

I was met by a smile from the warden and, after a hot shower, felt almost relaxed. The rooms were smaller than in the previous hostels and the residents were even entrusted with carpeted floors. Mountain fatigue left very few free-staring members around the place. The sole occupant in the 'Quiet Room' could have been an exception. As I passed the door he appeared to be staring at television in the corner of the room. I went in to see if the news was on. There was no news, in fact there was no television, and the piece of wall that he was so intent on watching couldn't hold my attention for long. I left to cycle over to the hotel.

Raasay from the doorway of ruined house at Applecross

Torridon to Gairloch

Surviving breakfast without talking to anyone was proving to be difficult, especially in a hostel where open plan kitchen/dining areas encourage uninvited mingling amongst the boiling kettles. There was only one virulent conversationalist this morning who possessed sufficient skill to sustain a one-way conversation which required no responses or even eye contact from his verbal victim. He sat alone, surrounded by upturned chairs, delivering a speech to the back of another inmate who occasionally grunted acknowledgement several tables away. I kept my face close to the muesli and wished that I knew some words in Norwegian. All the same, when I was washing up, I was caught and I lost valuable minutes of my life nodding to 'I'll tell you something funny ... ' There followed a lengthy tale, something to do with a dirty dishcloth in a hostel in the Outer Hebrides.

The road to Diabaig, Torridon

I rolled out the bike and headed up the north side of Loch Torridon along the single-track road which ends nine miles further on at Diabaig. From there I was planning to take the hill path or track for the eight miles round the coast to Redpoint on the west of this Gairloch headland. It would take me past the remote Youth Hostel of Craig which can only be reached by this path. From the village of Torridon, the road follows the loch shore before climbing up through the forest to cross the bridge over Coire Mhic Nobuil, the river that flows down from the high mountain corries on Beinn Alligin and Liathach. The footpath that leads onto these hills starts at the cluster of Scots pines next to the bridge. Although I was tempted to follow it on this beautiful day, I kept cycling, head down, for Diabaig.

Coming out of the trees, the road stretches high on the hillside with views across towards Applecross. At the small group of houses at Alligin Shuas, the road turns north and climbs steeply to cross Bealach na Gaoithe, The Pass of the Winds. Even if you were to go no further, it is worth coming up the road to see this misplaced alpine pass. Near the top, I stopped to look back at the ice-carved peaks of Torridon. The local post bus passed by and I watched it wind its way slowly back down the hill like a scene from a Postman Pat book. The views to the west suddenly opened up as the road emerged from the steep-sided crags guarding Bealach na Gaoithe and a greener landscape came as a surprising contrast to the wildness of the last few miles. I was relieved to see that the land on the cross-country route to Redpoint looked relatively flat. It was a rapid descent to the shores of Loch Diabaig, trapped in the hills above the village, and then down even more steeply into the sculpted bowl of cliffs that surround Lower Diabaig. This remarkable village seems out of place here, forgotten in its secret cove and hidden in an amphitheatre of rock and forest. At the road end, just beyond Diabaig, I found the dishcloth storyteller taking his walking boots out of his car. It could prove to be an even tougher journey than I'd feared; I quickly shouldered the bike, found the small gate at the beginning of the path and took to my heels.

My pace soon slowed on the rough path as I made my way over the hills to Craig Youth Hostel, some three miles away, with the bicycle bumping along at my side. I looked across at the sun shining on the northern cliffs of Skye and thought how different it all could have appeared in the rain. Even in today's safer weather, I was still glad to reach the crest of a rise and see a solitary building nestling in the green valley of the river Craig far below me. As I neared the remote Youth Hostel, I noticed a young woman working at a table just in front of the house, preparing some vegetables. I wondered whether she would welcome my intrusion into her privacy. Not an eye was raised! I passed by on the lower path, feeling somewhat irrationally ignored by her silence.

Having dropped downstream too far, I had some difficulty finding a place to cross the river Craig. I eventually found a spot where it looked narrow enough to risk leaping over to a boulder on the far bank. It would be a delicate manoeuvre and I had to rely on the bike, balanced precariously on my shoulder, behaving itself. But it let me down, waiting until my leading foot had just landed on a rock on the far bank before the handlebars swung round wildly, slamming the front wheel into my face. The impact of the rough tread of the tyre on my nose led to my next mistake – an unwise decision to let go my hold of the clump of heather on the far bank. I began to fall backwards and was nearly strangled by the frame of the bike which had slipped round my neck. I just managed to regain my balance and wrestle free. What an indignity to be attacked by your own bike! Even worse, was the possibility that she, who had just now so calmly ignored me, had seen it all happening.

I struggled up the steep bank and joined the path again. From the top of the next ridge, I could see all the way along the coast to the sands at Red Point. Many years ago I had started walking round the coast from Redpoint towards Torridon. The weather had been too bad to get very far and I had often wondered where the path went. It was now very satisfying to find out at last that it led to where I was now standing.

Red Point, where I could rejoin the tarmac on the road to Gairloch, remained in sight although it never seemed to get any nearer. The path was good enough, but rocky, and there was only one very short stretch which was flat enough to cycle. Pushing and pulling an increasingly heavy bike over six long miles was wearying.

Although less dramatic than earlier landscapes, the open moor offered many attractions – if only I could get to that beach.

Tiredness made me question again the spoiling of a fine walk by dragging a bicycle along, even though I knew that it was the only way that my route could continue along the coast. Clearly, crossing open countryside was taking a long time and although I would reach Gairloch that day, I began to think that Cape Wrath with a bike was likely to prove beyond me. This was a depressing conclusion although probably quite realistic. I had hoped to take three hours to cross from Torridon to Red Point but it was five and a half hours from leaving Diabaig that I finally reached those cream sands. The smooth expanse of beach, freshly swept by the outgoing tide, was, gratifyingly even more beautiful than it looked from a distance, and just the kind of place where the walrus and the carpenter had taken a stroll.

Having spent all those hours pushing the bike, I was very glad to get a seat on it and began pedalling along the track, even though it meant turning into wind and weariness again. It was a very slow cycle back along that road I had driven down in the mist all those years ago. For the first time, I could see clearly why this dead-end road was so popular. On the right, looking back towards Torridon, the red sandstone peaks rose up from the moor, whilst out at sea, the distant islands were lining up in the Hebrides. It wasn't difficult to pick out the hills of Harris and the flatness of its northern neighbour, Lewis. Uist and Benbecula were more difficult to identify in the chain of blue shapes on the horizon. Surrounded by extraordinary beauty, spending most of my time staring at gravel chips and tarmac as the wind kept my head down at wheel, was a real shame.

About to dismount and walk up a steep rise, I briefly formed a piece of photographic foreground for someone taking a picture of the seascape. When I noticed a man pointing a camera at me, I continued cycling, a fine display of vanity keeping me in the saddle!

There was some shelter from the wind in store for me when I reached Badachro on the shores of Loch Gairloch. This picturesque village, tucked in a tiny bay, is guarded by a ring of islands and has a leisurely-paced look about it. The Badachro Inn, built at the water's edge, was quiet and the handful of boats in the bay swayed gently at their moorings: a place for 'No good boyo' in his rowing boat whiling away an afternoon with a 'I don't know who's up there and I don't care' attitude. From here onwards, the road winds its way in and out of birch and oak woods until it reaches the main road just south of Charlestown.

Bay near Badachro on the Gair Loch

The first rain of the week began falling as I cycled into Gairloch in the late afternoon. I was tired and unimpressed by the amusement centre and take-away Balti curry signs. Even the name Gairloch Sands hinted at the emptiness of this straggle of townships. It looked like a failed resort of the 1950s and some of the postcards had pictures showing old Austin/Morris cars on the streets of Gairloch.

There seemed to be little chance of finding anywhere to stay on the road to Poolewe and the tourist office staff were not even very confident that I would find somewhere in Gairloch either because only one B&B would entertain a 'single'.

'What's it like?' I asked.

'Well, we've had no complaints,' was the reply.

Praise indeed, and I rushed off to find this 'total destination resort'. In the circumstances, the faded green and mauve décor in the bedroom of the one available room could be endured for one night. 'Will you be wanting a normal breakfast?' the slippered landlady asked. None of this vegetarian nonsense here and she returned to her kitchen presumably to start wrestling with the bacon for the overnight fry.

The hills of Torridon

Bay from Badachro on the Gair Loch

Gairloch to Ullapool

Although I had slept well, I awoke tired and doubtful about my chances of getting as far as Ullapool, especially when I noticed that the wind continued blowing strongly from the north. Mrs Slippers was in little doubt, however, so with her cheerful 'You'll be lucky' ringing in my ears, I slunk out of Gairloch. All chances of reaching Cape Wrath by Saturday would be lost if I failed to make it to Ullapool in one day. Having foolishly overlooked the fact that buses would not run on the Lord's Day, my original plan of reaching the Cape on Sunday and catching the post bus back to Lairg had to be abandoned. Now I had to try and gain a day somehow if I wanted to make the train connection for Edinburgh.

It was a slow climb away from the coast and up across the wild mountainous terrain, past numerous small lochs and rocky crags on the road to Poolewe. This was a harsh place to live where only the toughest animals survive. Even the sheep were fierce, I thought, judging by the one at the side of the road repeatedly head-butting a fence post to pass the time of day. I cycled cautiously by, trying to avoid catching its eye. Then I noticed that it had somehow managed to get its curled horn entwined in the wire of the fence. My first instinct was to pretend that I hadn't seen it, but my proven skills with sheep handling would not let me pass by. At least this time I was fairly sure that I would be able to deal with the right end and approached it for a closer look. The tangle of horn and fence wire resembled one of those metal puzzles that only pull apart if you get both bits in exactly the right position. In this case, whilst one part was metallic and relatively static, the other piece was fleecy, frantic and furious. I didn't know that sheep growled and I jumped back somewhat daunted by the snarling beast. I looked back at the road in case there was anyone about to laugh at my embarrassment – or would notice if I left. After several attempts at twisting the wire and horn, I succeeded in releasing the animal. It scampered free across the heather, and stopped. The sheep then slowly turned to look at me as if to say 'thank you.' Like hell it did!

I was glad to reach Poolewe and began to feel slightly more hopeful of making it to Ullapool. It is here, where Loch Maree so nearly reaches the sea, that Osgood MacKenzie created his sub-tropical garden at Invercwe which I had last visited many years ago on a grey September day. Today, the beautiful warren of a garden, a surprise at every corner, was bathed in the scent of azaleas. Paths wound their way among the ferns, between bushes of bamboo and under trees of magnolia and eucalyptus. Some of the huge rhododendrons were creaking with blossom in keeping with their tranquil surroundings. The Chelsea football fans' old chant of 'Osgood is good' came to mind. One can only marvel at the great patience of the garden's designer. I think I would have settled for a Leylandei hedge and some lobelia. Come to think of it, I have.

The breathtaking views from the road north out to the open sea made up for the very few glimpses of Loch Ewe on offer from the gardens. Also breathtaking was the hilly road, steep at first and keeping to the contours of the hillside for several miles, before descending to the road junction at Aultbea. I wasn't expecting to see a naval base here and was further confused by the strange-looking names of the local villages. Where did a name like Drumchork come from? Then there was Mellon Charles and his brother Mellon Udrigle further north. Although the croft farming at Aultbea probably deserved a closer look, I continued on the windswept road, crossing the neck of the Rubha Mòr peninsula to reach the shores of Gruinard Bay at the village of Laide.

The skies had grown dark and rain was threatening but the greyness of the day somehow added to the grandeur of Gruinard Bay. I stopped for some time and gazed out to sea across the scattering of islands from nearby Gruinard to the distant Summer Isles and beyond to the Atlantic. Here was an uninterrupted view up the western coast of Scotland and the end was literally almost in sight. I could now pick out the familiar outline of the Sutherland hills crowding the distant horizon. The shape of Suilven was unmistakable and then there was

Canisp and Quinag, and was that snow on Ben More Assynt? As a hillwalker, I can't resist the guessing of mountains and continue to be surprised at just how frequently I am wrong: unless of course, I'm with someone who doesn't know better.

Although Gruinard Island had been infected by anthrax from germ warfare tests carried out during the Second World War, I can't pretend that this sad fact spoilt the view from this cliff-top road. On reaching the top of a rise, the tarmac surface ahead of me disappeared, the road dropped out of sight and I found myself staring across a vast chasm of mountain crags. These sombre hillsides, gashed by streams of white water, tumbled down to a beach of clean pink sand where the river Gruinard flowed into the sea. To the south and east the landscape was becoming more savage as the road skirted round the edge of the Fisherfield wilderness. This is a wild and remote area of rock-crested mountains which includes An Teallach, one of the most impressive hills on the Scottish mainland. There was so much to look at and yet, in what seemed like no time at all, I was free-wheeling down the side of Little Loch Broom, heading for Dundonnell.

It was two o'clock in the afternoon and because, for the first time for two days, I was making faster progress than expected, I stopped for coffee at the Dundonnell Hotel. All was well with the world and I sank back into the depth of a cushioned armchair in the residents' lounge, taking my pick of the National Geographical Magazines and changing seats several times just to slouch in different positions. The other reason for feeling so pleased with myself was that I had phoned Altnaharrie Inn and the owner had agreed to let me use the small passenger ferry to cross over Loch Broom to Ullapool. This meant that I could avoid the twenty-four mile detour south along the Destitution Road to Braemore, and take the much more direct route across the peninsula between Loch Broom and Little Loch Broom.

Shortly after leaving the hotel, I turned left off the main A832 and onto the single-track road signposted to Badrallach. I then must have taken a wrong turning at some point because I ended up in a maze of estate tracks that criss-crossed a wood of beech and sweet chestnut. Eventually, after crossing a suspended footbridge, rolling at every step, I found my way back onto the main road again and headed northwards, up onto the open hillside. There was a long climb ahead of me now, this time to over 750 feet. I stopped frequently to look back at An Teallach towering over Dundonnell as trails of smoking mist drifted across its snow-filled corries.

A couple of hundred yards further on, I found the small gate on the right to the track down to the shores of Loch Broom. I understand that the owner of the Altnaharrie Inn drives up this steep track to collect supplies. As I struggled to avoid large boulders and falling over the handlebars, I couldn't see how he ever made it up to the top. After several hundred feet of swerving and juddering, I arrived unscathed at the tranquil waterside setting of a posh restaurant adorned with a smooth lawn and cottage-flower garden. The diners were ferried across Loch Broom from Ullapool in a small boat and by contacting the Inn, it might be possible to arrange a lift across the loch. The boat was just about to leave on its short crossing as I arrived. Especially on a sunny afternoon, barely a ripple on the water and the town stretching out on a small headland to meet you, there is no better way to arrive.

The pier and harbour were busy as usual, but today, the whole place seemed particularly noisy after days spent in the quiet of the countryside. It is an attractive town with parallel streets of whitewashed houses and unlike some of the one-street villages in Scotland, there is a sense of purpose in the way it has been laid out. It was planned and built by the British Fisheries' Society in the late eighteenth century for herring fishing. Whilst this industry has long disappeared in many places, Ullapool has survived with some fishing and a lot of trawling for tourists, many taking the ferry over to Lewis and the other Outer Hebridean islands. The Youth Hostel in the centre of town, overlooking the harbour front, has an air of normality about it. As the warden had lost the keys to the high-technology till, no one could book in or out until she found them. I was becoming worryingly accustomed to hostel-life and soon embarked upon the unpacking and re-packing rucksack routine to while away some time.

I set out for a walk hoping to buy some film. When the Ceilidh Bookshop had none left, I thought about having a drink in the Ceilidh Hotel, and perhaps a meal in the Ceilidh Restaurant. I even enquired about the cost of staying a night in the upmarket bunkhouse called, somewhat surprisingly, the Ceilidh Club. I was tempted to visit the Ceilidh Place, the birthplace of Ceilidh pool, but I found a seat at the window of the Ferry Boat Inn instead and became gently mulled by some glasses of red wine and the view across the still waters of Loch Broom.

The loch and sky turned bright reddish-purple as the low rays of the dying sun streamed up Loch Broom from the west. I took a walk down to the shore by the campsite and along to the pier to watch the fishing boats unload their catch before returning to the hostel for an early night. Surprised at how quiet the place was, even though there were several people about, I made myself a cup of chocolate and sat in the dining area listening to the death rattle of a sweet wrapper.

Boats at Ullapool

Ullapool to Kylesku

I was woken by the rustle of rucksacks as early morning hostellers started their first pack of the day. I lay for a while, shrunk-wrapped in my sleeping bag, and waited for my skin to un-crease itself. There was time to reflect on last night's heroic decision to have that third glass of red wine and wonder why other people in sleeping bags always look so peaceful. Much of my night was spent wrestling with the bag to avoid strangulation before eventually dozing off, wound up like an Egyptian mummy and lying balanced on a folded wrist. As I unhinged my wrist and removed my elbow from my groin, a quick glance through the curtains revealed blue sky. I got up and joined the rustlers.

Breakfast made me feel bright enough to look forward to the day's cycle through Assynt. My original plan had been to leave the main A835 at Strath Kannaird, a few miles north of Ullapool, and take the coastal track around the southern slopes of Ben Mòr Coigach to join up with the road from Achiltibuie. I had been advised against trying to carry a bike plus rucksack along this steep route. My instinct was to ignore this, no doubt sound advice, until I remembered my tired 'trackle' along the path to Red Point. Consequently, I opted to stay on tarmac instead and take the minor road to Lochinver by the shores of Loch Lurgainn. This sad compromise significantly improved my chances of reaching Cape Wrath on Friday. The road along Loch Lurgain also passes by Stac Pollaidh, a magical wedge of rock soaring skywards above the loch. You can almost hear the dragons' roar. In fact I nearly fell off my bike when I ducked to avoid the blast of engine exhaust as a dragon jet flew low overhead. This is a raw landscape unlike any other area in Scotland and looks as if it belongs to a bygone age in a distant land. The further I pedalled through the wild countryside, the more my curiosity arose about the forces which had shaped this fractured west coast.

My main difficulty lay in a failure to grasp the concept that landscapes can change so dramatically over great stretches of time. It is the very sense of permanence about mountains which is part of their appeal. The possibility of such transformation became clearer once I began to appreciate the relatively fragile nature of the earth's surface, a thin crust floating on a large globe of heated metallic porridge. In places, sections of the crust collide and are forced upwards, forming mountain ranges like folds in a piece of ruffled cloth.

Apparently some thousand million years ago the surface of 'Scotland' was located below sea level at the equator. A mere 600 million years later, it had drifted north and the Highlands of Scotland were being forced up as part of a great 'Caledonian' collision. Slowly, well over a good year or two anyway, these Caledonian mountains, once possibly as high as the Himalayas, were eroded by ice, wind and rain and the core of their eruptions – the volcanic rock granite – exposed. The line of folding of these ancient mountains led to the 'grain' of the Scottish landscape which runs in a north-east/south to west direction.

The land mass of Scotland then sank below the surface of the sea only to rise up again as one block some thirty million years ago. The block was tilting slightly to the east and the high ridge of Scotland ran in a line north-south, close to the west coast. This is the line today which represents the watershed of the country and rivers flowed in the cracks or fault lines which had been caused by the early folding of the landscape, along the north-east to south-west grain. The ice age of two million years ago speeded up erosion with the flow of the glaciers fragmenting the west coast by cutting ice channels, separating Skye, Mull and many of the west-coast islands from the mainland.

As the ice age came to an end, sea levels rose and the former glaciated valleys on the west coast were flooded, creating the fjord-like sea lochs. At the same time the flooding of the channels and minches resulted in areas of high ground being separated from the mainland, creating the necklaces of islands on the west coast.

Only the far north-west of Scotland, in a line running from Kyle of Lochalsh to Durness, resisted the Caledonian uprising. Here a hard rock shield of gneiss, an ancient volcanic rock usually only found

Caledonian MacBrayne ferry leaving Kilchoan

The bridge at Kylesku

Gruinard Bay

Loch Ailort and the hills of Moidart

St Abb's Head

Sea stacks at Duncansby

Skye from Applecross

Shieldaig, Loch Torridon

The white sands of Morar

Torridon

Ullapool

Hermitage Castle

Sandwood Bay

Stac Pollaidh

Quinag

A track through Lossie Forest

East-coast sunset at Pennan and angry seas at Ardnamurchan Point

deep in the earth's crust, was covered by a thick layer of sandstone and remained unmoved. The top layer of red sandstone, some three thousand feet thick, is thought to have been formed from sand deposited when Scotland lay at the bottom of the equatorial sea – remember all those minutes ago? But now most of the sandstone has been swept away leaving the relic mountains of Sutherland, including Suilven and Stac Pollaidh, standing proud above their basement of barren gneiss. But I digress.

So, after all my reckless over-simplification of Scotland's west-coast geology, I wasn't much further along the road, having stopped frequently to watch the sunlight move across the sharp cone of Stac Pollaidh. I can never pass this mountain without attempting at least one photograph. I snapped at it when the whole of its rock-crested ridge was lit up by the sun and again when it was half in shade. I took another photograph with the chrome yellow gorse flowering in the foreground and even one with the jet fighter overhead. Unfortunately, as usual, once developed, the photographs all had that 'missed me again' look about them.

I followed the Achiltibuie road by the side of the still waters of Loch Lurgainn and Loch Bad a' Ghaill before turning off to cross over the western slopes of Stac Pollaidh towards Inverkirkaig. It was a steady climb to the crest of the ridge. Looking back from the top of this four-hundred-foot climb was the cathedral spire of Stac Pollaidh and, to the north, I gazed across a vast floor of twisted gneiss rock bestrewn with hundreds of silvered lochans. Rising out of the barren wasteland was the great mountain pillar of Suilven.

As I sat looking at this ancient scene, the clouds gathered overhead and a hailstorm passed over. I felt cold and slightly intimidated by the sense of remoteness and lack of shelter in this unforgiving terrain. The steepness of the descent meant that I was back down to sea level and relative warmth in a matter of minutes. This road was magnificent, full of contrasts as it carved its way through the rocks and lochans and then burrowed deep into the greenery of steep, wooded glens where swarms of lemon-cream primroses covered the sheltered valley floor. The brief glimpses of the sea were worth waiting for, particularly at Enard Bay where the narrow road emerged from its woodland cover and out onto a narrow ledge curving round the silent cove.

The scene was very idyllic, especially with spring flowers at the roadside sparkling in the sunshine. Unfortunately, all this beauty failed to add any sparkle to my legs which were tiring rapidly on the switchback of ups and downs. Lochinver seemed a long time in coming but I eventually crossed the river Kirkaig and entered Sutherland and the area known as Assynt. The scenery here is very different to other parts of Scotland and many of the place names, like Assynt and Elphin, have an unusual ring to them, evidence of the two-hundred-year Norse occupation. To the Vikings occupying Orkney and Shetland, this part of Scotland represented the 'south lands' and hence the name Sutherland. I stopped for a brief rest at the small village of Inverkirkaig to summon up enough energy for the three or four miles to the bright lights of Assynt at Lochinver. By now, even the easiest gradient required a lot of pushing down on the pedals.

Lochinver is not one of the prettiest towns in the Highlands and, like Mallaig, it takes its sheds seriously – hardly surprising for one of the main fishing ports on the west coast. Anyway, when a town has a mountain as impressive as Suilven nearby, visitors don't need to spend too much time peering at the pier. The main shopping street is at the other end of the bay and I had lunch in a smart, new restaurant which offered an exotic selection of hot pies. I finally settled for *Boeuf Bourguignon* and it settled for me. We settled near the window, the pie and I, and stared at each other for a while. It was a memorable lunch.

The weather had changed by the time I left the restaurant and the skies were darkening as the first drops of rain began to fall. I allowed myself the luxury of a light panic on discovering that one of the bolts holding the bottom of the bike rack in place had come off. I hastily cycled round to a ship's chandlers-ironmongery-looking shop near the pier which I had noticed earlier. The man behind the counter listened in unsmiling silence to my garbled request, took the bolt, and disappeared into the back of the shop with a 'maybe'. What a contrast to the urban customer-care approach where you're greeted with smiles and apologies to explain that 'They don't make these F4s any more'. This monosyllabic sales assistant returned with a bolt he had taken the trouble to cut down to the right size for me. Lochinver was rising in my estimation despite the now bucketing rain. I went for some shelter in the Tourist Information Office, hoping that they could persuade me to 'corrupt' my day's route even further by suggesting that I took the more direct route inland to Kylesku. Once again, I wasn't let down because the more picturesque coastal route had very 'limited' accommodation. Completing my compromise of this very beautiful peninsula, I headed due east out of Lochinver along the main A837 back inland towards Skiag Bridge. In terms of my aim to cover as much of the mainland coast during my journey, this decision was indefensible, especially when it meant missing out places as beautiful as Achmelvich and the Stoer peninsula. But there again, it was raining. And after thirty miles, tiredness was now playing its usual dominant role in decision-making.

Although the main route out of Lochinver lacks the scenic grandeur of the coast, cycling on a road that was relatively straight and flat, after the tortuous twists and climbs on the way to Inverkirkaig, was most pleasant. The road climbs gradually for four miles or so with fine views to the south along the whole trailing ridge of Suilven. I spotted a cyclist in the distance coming towards Lochinver, the first one I could remember seeing out on the open road for three days. He or she was sufficiently far away to give me time to rehearse my vocal quip. Would it be 'Hi' or perhaps risk a 'Not a bad day'? Surely there must be something wiser to say to demonstrate the bond between fellow cyclists on a lonely road? As he got closer, I realised that there were certain differences between our approaches to cycling. He was probably on a day out from Harrogate, looking super-light in racing shorts and singlet. I was more in the heavyweight division, a kind of wobbling waterproofed baggage on two wheels. Undaunted, I lifted my head to establish the briefest of eye contact to preface my greeting. I was just in time to see a thigh muscle flash past me. I think his knees were connected to his chin in some way to maximise pedal lift because otherwise I'm sure he would have welcomed some roadside banter. Simply lifting his head for a second would have been enough. My well-rehearsed 'Hi' would have to wait for another occasion. No point in wasting words unnecessarily.

The remaining six miles to Skiag Bridge were along the shores of Loch Assynt. The colours of the landscape brightened during the afternoon as the clouds began to break up and the sunshine returned. To my left, the lower slopes of Quinag remained steely grey but there was a splash of bright green vegetation around Inchnadamph at the far end of the loch. The gaunt ruins of Arbreck Castle stood at the edge of Loch Assynt's blue waters and in the distance, rising up behind Inchnadamph, were the snow-clad ridges of Ben More Assynt and Conival. I turned left at Skiag Bridge onto the main road, heading north along the A894 to Kylesku. There was now a steady climb for the next three miles to cross over the 850 foot high pass between Quinag on my left and Glas Bheinn to the east. It was a tiring push and pedal but the sun was on my back and I knew that it was the last climb of the day, providing of course I could find somewhere to stay around Kylesku. The close-up views of the rock-buttressed ridges of Quinag also kept me from feeling too weary. But it was the view from the crest of the road northwards down to Kylesku across Loch Glencoul and out to the open sea at Eddrachillis Bay that made me stop and gaze. The northern coastline lay exposed and Cape Wrath at long last looked within reach.

It was now downhill all the way to Kylesku on the shores of Loch a' Chairn Bhàin. There were only a few houses clustered round the harbour and I suspected that I could have some difficulty finding accommodation for the night. I had a list of B&B places to contact and after a few phone calls managed to negotiate a night in the neighbouring village of Unapool, just a mile or so back up the road. I say negotiate, because there was some reluctance to take in a 'single' and it was a relief when the proprietors finally relented. Unapool House is built on high ground with beautiful views across Loch Glencoul to the surrounding gallery of rocky hills. The steep slopes of Quinag tower over the back garden. This was a good place to stay; and not just because the owners invited me in for a drink later in the evening.

The local Hotel at Kylesku, obviously a well-known local eating-place, offered a very lavish menu. I couldn't decide on a main course and with reckless abandon, had the mushroom soup and a pastry pudding instead. It was a pity that the bar was swamped by a shoal of large men with loud accents. They were on a fishing trip and staying a few miles up the coast in Scourie. Even ordering a round of drinks was brought to the attention of all.

'So is that a pint, Piffer, or are you sticking to the G and Ts?'

'So that's three pints of your best bitter, landlord. Two G and Ts and four Scotches; better make them large ones.'

'Oh, do you want to make that a malt Charles?

'Now come on Froggie, stop mucking about and say what … '

Outside, the red sandstone buttresses of Quinag blazed in the light of the setting sun and I left to cycle across the Kylesku Bridge for a better view.

Kylesku to Kinlochbervie

The small dining room overlooking the loch was a very pleasant place to sit and collect my meagre early morning thoughts. Surrounded by pottery and geraniums, I sat alone and enjoyed a superb breakfast. Even though this is how I always imagined a B&B could be like, for some reason I felt just a bit like an intruder. Perhaps the fact that there had been a certain reluctance to let me have the room in the first place and the owner's view that cyclists 'must be mad' made me feel slightly out of place. I took extra care not to spill crumbs on the tablecloth and managed to leave without breaking anything. Some day, I will return – in a Volvo!

The bridge at Kylesku, an elegant structure with clean lines of arching concrete, was built in the 1980s to replace the small car ferry that used to cross on a chain between Kylesku and Kylestrome. That short crossing of just 300 yards made this corner of Scotland seem far more remote than it does today. The bridge looks as if it has been designed for one of those old 'I want to break free' adverts with the silver car driven by a silky-haired model escaping to the freedom of the wild country.

I was making slightly slower and less elegant progress, in no particular hurry, as I headed north into the area known as the Forest of Reay. My next planned night stop, Kinlochbervie, was only twenty-five miles away which meant I could take it easy and save some energy for the next day's crossing of the Cape. Even though the main road steers clear of the coast for the first few miles from Kylesku, there are some glimpses of the sea and the islands of Eddrachillis Bay. I stopped to look across Badcall Bay, sprinkled with tiny islands, some no bigger than large rocks. There is something quite strange about this bay which looks as if it was flooded yesterday rather than a million years ago.

From Badcall, it is only a couple of miles to Scourie, the base for the stockbroker fishing fleets, where the hotel car parks had more than their local quota of four-wheel-drive Tonka trucks. The village houses are spread thinly across the rocky terrain, but with a shop/Post Office as well the hotels, Scourie is, for this part of Scotland, a busy metropolis.

The A894 road heads east from Scourie, crossing more of the gnarled rock wasteland on the way to Laxford Bridge. About halfway, there is a road on the left to Tarbet on the coast and from here you can take a boat across to Handa Island, a nature reserve and bird sanctuary. There's a bridge at Laxford Bridge, over one of the finest salmon rivers in Scotland, but not much else to match its prominence on road maps. It was, however, the final turning point north for me as I joined the A838 Lairg to Durness road for the next five miles across the hills to Rhiconich. The wind was still blowing into my face and it was a slow crossing of rock and lochan-strewn gneiss landscape. It looked as if a new road was being built over the high pass and it was whilst I was cycling on the rough, temporary road surface that the back wheel started to judder. I knew without looking that it was a puncture. Nevertheless, I still gave myself the satisfaction of swearing when I saw the flattened rim of the tyre.

Needless to say, I was well organised and carrying a spare inner tube with me. Within a remarkably short time I was very complacently pumping up the replacement. It was such a simple task that there was no need to waste time checking for other problems, even though the wheel did seem to be catching slightly. Better to leave this isolated hillside and get down to Rhiconich, I thought.

It could have been as far as two, or even three hundred yards before the juddering returned and this time I heard that deflating hiss. I doubled up on the swearing, using curses as both nouns and adjectives. It wasn't as if I was surprised! Whilst mending the first puncture, I knew that no mechanical problem could be so simple: no vehicle repair that only needed to be done once. Years ago, when I drove around in ageing second-hand cars, I used to spend weeks carrying out relatively simple repairs, never succeeding in correcting faults at the first attempt. Surely I could manage to repair a bicycle puncture?

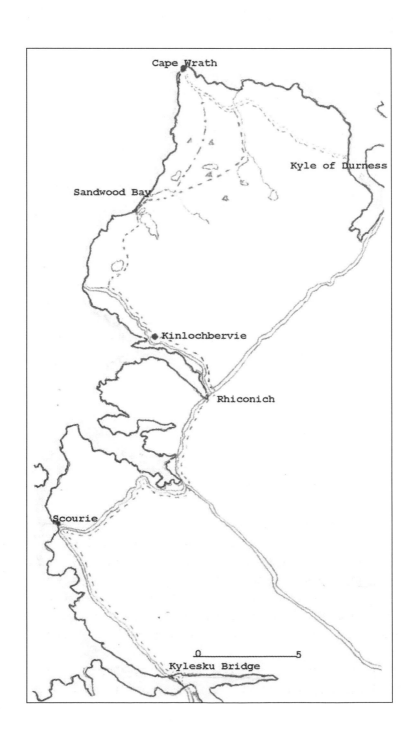

Cape Wrath

Kyle of Durness

Sandwood Bay

Kinlochbervie

Rhiconich

Scourie

0 ———————— 5

Kylesku Bridge

I had now run out of new inner tubes and, as I couldn't find the leak on the first one either, I pushed the limping bicycle the two miles downhill to the remote village of Rhiconich. It is amazing how the simplest of faults like a puncture renders a bicycle useless. I left the bike un-padlocked outside the hotel when I went inside to order coffee. If someone stole it, that would teach it a lesson!

I found a sink in the hotel toilet and pumped up the injured tube to check for bubbling leaks. I'm not sure how anybody passing the door of the toilet would have interpreted the noise of a bicycle pump from within. My inner tube could have been a big disappointment.

Discreetly, I managed to use the puncture repair kit whilst finishing off my coffee at the table in the restaurant, that is, as discreetly as anyone can be when repairing a puncture in a restaurant. Thinking that it might be difficult to bring the bicycle wheel into the hotel without attracting some comment, I left to finish the repair outside. Anyway, sitting on the pavement gave me the chance to chat to passers by.

'Puncture, eh?'

''Fraid so.'

This conversation, used with some success several times before setting out for the shores of Loch Inchard, had a certain predictability about it. It was good to get back in the saddle and realise that it was only four miles to Kinlochbervie where I would stay the night. Loch Inchard was the last of the thirty large sea lochs I had travelled round since reaching the shores of Loch Ryan at Stranraer several years ago. It forms the south-western shore of the final headland on the west coast, Cape Wrath, and like the rest of the sea lochs north of Torridon, it follows the grain of the ancient gneiss rocks. It is the change in direction of fault lines that makes it look as if this north-western tip of Scotland was lifting its head to look at something, perhaps Greenland, where some of its mountains came from.

I didn't feel very confident that the puncture repair would hold. The clicking sound which was still there wasn't worth wasting too much time worrying about, especially when the sun came out from behind the clouds and brightened the green crofting lands at the lochside. I began to brighten up as well – until I had to brake at a sharp corner. Immediately the clicking stopped and my saddle lowered that crucial inch. The juddering had returned. There was now more pressure in my head than in the back tyre and no variation of swear words would ease it. I have been told that if you find yourself in a deep hole, the first rule is to stop digging. I prefer to swear instead but I was running out of expletives and ideas. I had come too far now to give up and was prepared to walk to Cape Wrath if necessary, with or without my bike.

The road between Rhiconich and Kinlochbervie rises high above the loch with panoramic views back at the sculpted hills of Foinavon, Arkle and Ben Stack and out west to the open sea. It was a long push, walking downhill as well as up and I stopped at the shop at Badcall just in case there might be a tyre repair kit available. There wasn't, of course, but the shopkeeper used the opportunity to ask me some direct questions about where I was going and where I had come from. I liked this more direct conversational approach which missed out the 'turned out nice again' niceties. A short time later, I was very relieved to reach the top of the last rise and finally look down on Kinlochbervie.

The village itself is little more than a scattering of houses on the silent hillside above the noise and bustle of the large harbour and fish market on Loch Inchard. I found a sheltered wall out of the wind, not an easy thing to do in Kinlochbervie, and sat down on the pavement to mend some punctures. It was still only half-past three in the afternoon and as I had sufficient hours of daylight to mend several, I could relax and take my time. I had stopped digging! A calmer and closer look at the tyre and back brake revealed the cause of the problem. Part of the back brake block, which presses against the wheel rim when braking, had been ground down to a sharp ridge. This was rubbing against the side-wall of the rear tyre and had worn a hole in the side of the outer layer of thick rubber. The inner tube was bulging through this gap and every time I braked, the ridge on the brake block sliced a hole through it. Quite simple really!

I borrowed a spanner from the local garage and the mechanic suggested that the nearest place for a new tyre would be Inverness, nearly a hundred miles away. The position seemed hopeless. Having cycled all these miles from Portpatrick, it looked as if I wasn't going to make the last fifteen to Cape Wrath.

A young child, probably no more than eight, said 'hello' and smiled at me as he walked by. I was surprised by this reckless gesture. Hasn't he been told not to talk to strangers mending punctures? I soon realised that the adults also said 'hello' to strangers. No wonder the children acquired bad habits. Despite the tyres, I began to feel cheered by a village where people still talked openly to each other.

There was a B&B sign on 'The Roadside' opposite, and its owner, Mr Morrison, was one of the villagers who showed a passing interest in my puncture. His garden looked like a good place to repair tyres, certainly preferable to my piece of pavement. I took a room for the night. Mr Morrison provided a very welcome cup of tea and, even more importantly, some understanding of my desire to reach Cape Wrath on a bicycle. He wasn't entirely convinced of the feasibility of cycling there because there were no roads, not even a track beyond Sandwood Bay. However, he was familiar with this kind of folly having had a guest staying with him some years previously who had attempted to reach Cape Wrath on a motorbike. Apparently, the man had set off early one morning only to return a few hours later having failed to get beyond Sandwood Bay.

'So, did he just give up?' I asked.

'No, he got up even earlier the next day and set off again', explained Mr Morrison. Not very late that evening, he returned. Consequently, Mr Morrison was a bit more supportive of my cross-country cycle than I would have expected and even found a piece of thick rubber to seal up the gap in the tyre wall. As long as I didn't use the brakes, I could attempt to follow the route the next day.

Feeling a lot more hopeful, I cycled down to the harbour to see if the repair would hold. It did, and my spirits rose as I watched the fishing boats arrive to unload their catch. In contrast to the quiet stillness of the village above, the quayside was alive with the noise of circling gulls, boat engines, cranes and the harrying whine of forklift trucks. By the following night, Friday, nearly all the fishermen here would have left for their homes on the east coast of Scotland.

It was a beautiful evening, high pressure everywhere, and after a meal in the local hotel, I cycled up the next day's road for a couple of miles to watch the sun light up the surrounding hills. On my way back to Mr Morrison's, a gang of teenage boys came down the road towards me. When they seemed to fan out across the road I instinctively wondered whether this meant trouble. I passed through the group; one smiled and asked whether I was on holiday. 'Why do you come here? There's nothing to see except scenery.' For one thing, I thought, there are people who seem prepared to trust strangers. For some of us, this is a bit of a novelty.

I went to bed early because I had to be up at five o'clock next morning. My plan was to cycle as far as Sandwood Bay and then cross 'through the hill' as Mr Morrison described it, by following a path which eventually would join up with the road or track running from the Kyle of Durness to Cape Wrath. Day visitors to Cape Wrath cross the Kyle of Durness by a small open boat and then take a minibus along a track for the eleven miles to Cape Wrath. I was hoping to meet up with the minibus at midday at the Cape and I reckoned that it would take me a minimum of six hours to get there from Kinlochbervie. If I failed to meet up with the minibus at the lighthouse, I would be stranded.

Sleep did not come easily. Excitement and the ticking of clocks cracking their way through the silence of a Kinlochbervie night kept me awake. After all the time spent planning and pedalling, I was now at the very edge of the map, hoping at last to see those high cliffs.

Kinlochbervie to Cape Wrath

The tick-tock alarm clock lent to me by Mr Morrison made a terrible noise at five o'clock in the morning. Here was none of the electronic buzzing to snooze and soothe me into the day; it was more a fire bell sound to shock me out of bed. Still, I was looking forward to the day ahead, especially when I saw the early morning sunshine. I just hoped that I was strong enough to reach this remote corner of these isles: that, and enough air in the back tyre.

I tiptoed downstairs to the dining room of clocks and found that tables were set for half a dozen people. Did they come in last night or were the plates always there just in case? A brief look at the historical display of family photographs, a quick breakfast and I was out pedalling by half-past five.

Conditions were perfect with barely a cloud in the sky. Even the wind hadn't got up yet. I followed the single-track road going north from Kinlochbervie to the small village of Sheigra, enjoying the cold of the morning air and crisp views of a magnificent coast. I stopped at Oldshore More and looked back down the blue coastline to the warm, red hills of Quinag and beyond to Suilven at Lochinver. Away in the distance, on the other side of Eddrachillis Bay, the sun lit up a tall sea stack, perhaps the Old Man of Stoer, near Achmelvich.

Uncertain about the time it might take to reach Cape Wrath, I satisfied myself with a distant view of Oldshore More's beautiful sandy beach. I kept on pedalling, staying on the tarmac road past Blairmore and then, just before reaching the small crofting community of Sheigra, turned right onto the track that crosses the moor to Sandwood Bay. The good surface on the track for the first mile began to soften as it crossed the peat bogs of the open moor. It was fairly slow going carrying the bike across the badly eroded sections where the track had disappeared into black puddles of oozing peat.

Doubts about whether I was fit enough to make the cross-country route to the Cape began to grow in my mind. Carrying the bike and a rucksack a short distance over soft ground was exhausting, let alone reaching Sandwood Bay. Had it not been for the sunshine, I don't believe I would have had the perseverance to continue. Too tired to return the four miles across that boggy ground, the only way forward was northwards. I had expected this to be both the most difficult and the most exhilarating day of the whole journey and inevitably, my mood changed frequently over the next few hours. Just as I began to feel defeated by tiredness, I reached the top of a rise. Shouting with excitement, I looked down on the elegant curve of Sandwood Bay.

Sandwood Bay

Of all the beautiful beaches on the west coast, never have I seen one with the atmospheric quality as Sandwood. The ruined bothy on the edge of the neighbouring freshwater loch is said to be haunted by the ghost of a bearded sailor, whilst mermaids have been seen on the beach. Whatever about spirits, it is undoubtedly an inspiring place, especially at seven o'clock in the morning when the sun shines. The bright green of the surrounding grassy slopes leading down to the bay contrasted with the cream sands and a turquoise sea. The bay is carved out of the surrounding headland, low cliffs edging the northern end and the tall sea stack of Am Buachaille, the Herdsman, guarding the south shore. I kept a close eye on the breaking waves hopeful of seeing a mermaid as I cycled slowly across the soft sands.

Five minutes later, I was cursing my failure to scale those northern rocks with a bike on my back. Half way up, I collapsed exhausted. The rise ahead looked even steeper and I began to realise that if I couldn't even cope with the relatively short scramble up these low cliffs, I would never manage the next six miles. I left the bike behind some rocks and climbed to the top of the slope to see what lay ahead and although the ground certainly flattened out slightly, I still couldn't see over the top of the ridge. There were plenty more rocks to clamber over before I would reach the crest. It looked a hopeless task. I realised that I wasn't going to be physically strong enough to reach Cape Wrath if I had to carry the bike for long stretches. And anyway, what was the point? I made my way back down to find somewhere to conceal the bike. If I were to reach Cape Wrath, it would have to be on foot.

Abandoning my mountain bike after 480 miles left me close to tears. I tucked it behind a large rock and climbed slowly back up, dragged down by an overwhelming sense of failure. I didn't get too far before the command 'Keep going until you're on your knees' sprang to mind. Rock-by-rock, that bike was hauled up to the summit of the first ridge, with a stop every minute or so to get my breath back. Surely, this was just being plain stupid to say the least? After all, who would really care if I didn't reach my destination? Carefully weighing up all the hopes and expectations of friends, family, neighbours, and colleagues at work, I finally narrowed it down to there being just one person who would be really upset if I gave up. And he had a bike on his back.

The frequent stops to recover energy afforded opportunities to look back to Sandwood Bay. It looked even more impressive from above as the blue-green shallow waters caught the sunlight. Later, having reached the top of a rise where I couldn't see the bay at all and had begun to drop down to Strath Chaileach on the other side, I was in a happy state of mind.

Ahead lay several miles of wild moor, rising in places to form low-lying hills that appeared to bar the way to the north. Instead of taking the path to the Cape that follows the cliffs along the shore, I was planning to stay about half a mile inland to follow a more direct and less hilly route. I made my way down to the river in Strath Cailleach and found a place to cross. Although there was no sign of any recognisable path, it was slightly easier pushing the bike through the heather than over those rocks. I knew that I would have to climb to about 600 feet to 'go through the hill', as Mr Morrison had put it. That, thankfully, was still a few miles away. A large loch before then would be a useful landmark in barren wasteland. To my right, I could just see the remote bothy of Strath Cailleach, apparently inhabited by a sixty-year old 'hermit' who arrived from the south some twenty years earlier. I tried to imagine what it would be like to spend a dark winter alone in this wilderness: no electricity or mains water and a long walk once a fortnight to Kinlochbervie to collect essential supplies and some light refreshment.

There was no prospect of riding the bicycle at this stage. I tugged it over the peat and heather as I tried to work out where I was. Having to lift it over the larger peat hags made progress slow and I still could not see any sign of the loch. It was going to take me a long time to reach the north coast, and to make matters worse, the way ahead seemed to be all uphill. I stopped to check the compass. I was still heading in about the right direction, although slightly further east than I had expected. The sensible thing would have been to start bearing west but this would have meant crossing a steep ridge. Clearly, tiredness was making it more difficult to think rationally. Perhaps common sense requires more energy than instinctive folly? Either way, I had now convinced myself that my route lay straight ahead. It is always 'straight ahead' on these mindless occasions, even when walking in circles in the mist. Today, there was no mist to use as an excuse for getting lost on the struggle up to the top of a high ridge between two hills. I still hadn't seen the essential loch and there was a long way to go before I reached the planned hill crossing. Up through the rocks and heather I pushed a bike that was getting heavier by the minute as the slope grew steeper. While Sandwood Bay looked encouragingly small from the crest of the ridge, there was still no loch to be seen.

The first thing to do when lost is to refuse to accept it. It wasn't fear but a sense of shame that made me reluctant to face up to the disconcerting truth that I was alone and lost in the wild. Often, it is simply a question of re-interpreting the features of the map to match the appearance of the landscape around you. At other times, more extravagant reasoning is required: the absence of this particular loch could be caused by a summer drought. Now this loch is a great blue blob on the map, about a third of a mile wide. There was almost as much chance of the mountain ridge walking a mile to the east as there was of the loch evaporating in May. This conclusion, however, gave me a bit of irrational comfort as I began the steep descent from the ridge. At least I wasn't lost.

On dropping down about a hundred bumpy feet, I was able to see round to the left of the hill. There, to my great relief, was the loch. All four hundred yards of unevaporated water! The only problem was that it was either the wrong shape on the map (there I go again!) or it was another loch which should have been on my right? Nonetheless, it was a relief to see some water and I even thought that I could distinguish the northern coastline in the distance.

Once past the silent shores of the loch, the ground became flatter and boggier as I neared a river cutting through the moor. I was now following contours, paying little attention to the map and not bothering at all with the compass. These were either the tactics of a highly experienced walker whose instinct never failed him, or a very tired idiot pushing a bicycle for miles across a wilderness. The sight of two distant figures climbing the hillside on the far bank of the river cheered me and convinced me that they were crossing 'through the hill'. Still with a very long way to go, I was at the very least back on the planned route.

A Ministry of Defence 'DANGER KEEP OUT' sign on the far bank of the river came as a bit of a surprise. I ignored it, of course, dragging my bicycle up the steep slope on the far side of the river. I knew that the army used part of this area as a firing range and it was clearly marked on the ordnance survey map, but that was further east. Surely this sign had been misplaced? I did remember reading about the danger of unexploded bombs but I wasn't anywhere near a firing range. Then I saw another misplaced sign further along the bank. Time for another curse and then, for some unaccountable reason, I did something sensible and looked at the compass. Instead of the river running from east to west, which I had assumed it did, the compass showed that it was heading north. This seemed to suggest that I wasn't where I thought I was. Some might even loosely describe this as being lost. I still had the hill-crossing to make but at least I was heading northwards in the right direction.

This was my only comfort as I struggled to make my way along the riverbank, skirting the danger zone which now had begun to resemble a minefield, whatever that looks like. It was just after eleven o'clock in the morning, and if I was to get that lift to the ferry, I was running out of time. I was also becoming very tired again, having to stop frequently to swear and catch my breath. It was during one of these cursing comfort breaks that I spotted a line crossing the slopes. Still some distance away, it looked like a break in the heather. Perhaps it was a path of some kind.

The closer I got, the bigger the 'path' became until I could see that I was approaching a track which was running east-west. Then I realised that, somehow, I had finally reached the north coast. The track I was staring at with excited relief was the one crossing the Cape from the Kyle of Durness to Cape Wrath. I had come too far east and by crossing over an extra hill, I had added several miles to my route. But I had arrived!

It was so good to climb on the bicycle I had dragged all that way and to cycle those last four miles to the Cape. I caught my first real glimpse of the northern shore at the rocky cove of beautiful Kearvaig. At this stage, I didn't realise that I was still several miles from the Cape. It would be just round the next bend? The sense of elation at reaching the northern shore kept me going along the hilly and twisting track until that great moment when I saw that lighthouse, standing in all its solitary splendour, gleaming white in the midday sun.

The author at Cape Wrath

There were times when the journey up the west coast had been an endurance test. It had been planned simply for pleasure: to allow me to visit some of the most beautiful places imaginable. Cape Wrath, on a cloudless afternoon, where the horizon was marked by a darker shade of blue, was one of them. I walked round the lighthouse, revelling in simply being there. Until one of the lighthouse keepers came out for a chat, I had the place to myself. I took photographs of the cliffs running along the north coast. I took a picture of the massive rocks that stretch out into the Atlantic and, even worse, asked the lighthouse keeper to take a photograph of me sitting astride my bike!

An hour later, the minibus arrived with the day-trippers from Durness. More photographs (has this man no shame?) and a closer

look at Stevenson's lighthouse with its huge foghorn welded to the rock absorbed some more of my precious time here. I had some lunch in the warm sunshine and tried to imagine the remote Cape in the wrath of winter storms. It had taken me a long time to get here, to as grand a place as I had ever imagined.

Cape Wrath

I gazed across the blue horizon to the north, knowing that there was no more land between me and the North Pole. The name Wrath is a corruption of the Norse word meaning 'turning point', and for the Vikings, this meant heading south down the west coast. My eyes turned to look east along the gallery of cliffs that map out Scotland's northern edge. My journey would end here at the Cape, that is, until I saw those high cliffs. Could I negotiate an extension to my journey, visiting those northern shores and perhaps even crossing over to Orkney? I could blame my change of plans on the 'anatomy of restlessness', a theory, which I once heard described on the radio, that is based on the premise that modern man is descended from nomadic tribes. We've inherited an inborn desire to wander which conflicts with our present pre-occupation with the collection and guarding of possessions. Of course these nomads didn't have the chance to buy a Personal Equity Plan. I left with a last envious glance along those northern cliffs.

Part II

Along the Northern Edge

Cliffs along the Northern Edge from Cape Wrath

Durness to Tongue : 10 June 1995

It was the view along those northern cliffs and some restless winter evenings which led to my standing on Waverley Station platform at six o'clock in the morning, clutching two very large polythene bags. I had been trying since January to book the only bicycle place on the train from Edinburgh to Lairg without success as the ScotRail computer 'wasn't open for bookings'. When it did finally open its files for me in May, the space had already been allocated. The only option, therefore, was to bundle a dismembered mountain bike into an orange survival bag and, with the wheels partly hidden by a large Marks and Spencers' bag, disguise it as luggage. It was an undignified way for both of us to travel and to arrive, three train journeys, one post bus drive and nine hours later on the north coast in the gloom of a mist-drenched afternoon. When the sun shines, there are few finer places to arrive at than Durness. Today, the mist having drained all colour from the landscape, it felt like the end of beyond. The chill of the wind was even more depressing and, as I sat at the roadside in the centre of the

village unpacking my poly bags, I wondered what I was doing there. Perhaps I should have stopped at Cape Wrath whilst the sun shone.

Durness golf course

To cheer myself up, I cycled along to the Balnakeil graveyard. The lines of tombstone dominoes rose at odd angles from the sweep of bright, green turf in this cemetery on the edge of the bay. I took a photograph of the sombre ruined church (eighth century, I'm told) and wondered if graveyards become more interesting the older you got. Perhaps it is a good way of getting used to the idea, like Spike Milligan's advice to the elderly couple about where they should go on holiday: 'Not too far from a graveyard.'

I took a short walk along the pale sands of Balnakeil Bay which sweep northwards towards Faraid Head and had a quick look at the craft village at Balnakeil before heading back to Durness. In 1964, the derelict buildings of the site of a Ministry of Defence Early Warning Station were taken over by craftspeople. I think that the military may also have had a hand in the design of the wooden Nissen huts which make up the Youth Hostel at Smoo. There were no starers inside, in fact nobody at all, just an open door and the familiar smell of damp muesli.

Cemetery at Balnakeil

I climbed down the steps to the beach at Smoo to see a spectacular limestone cave. This huge black cavern, 130 feet wide and 50 feet high, was most inspiring. A walkway takes you to the start of the water-filled second chamber and while it is possible to take a boat into the inner chambers, the outer cave is more than sufficient.

Back in the hostel, it was still quiet in the lounge/kitchen area. Only Bill Eckersalt came in to wash up some of his tupperware containers and then he was off for an early night. As I had thought that he was a Bill Eckersalt as soon as I saw him, I was pleased to see that my guess was confirmed by the name on his thermos. I began to wonder why death had been so much on my mind as I crossed the parade ground to the dormitory block.

The wind from the north made it a cold start to the cycle on the narrow single-track road along the north coast. I stopped frequently to enjoy the views out to sea and across to the high cliffs of Whiten Head further along the coast. The cloud base was high and because I hoped to climb Ben Hope on my way to Tongue, it was encouraging to see that only the tops of the hills were still hidden in mist.

View from the Kyle of Tongue towards Ben Hope

The full benefit of the following wind was with me when the road turned south at the entrance to Loch Eriboll, an impressive fiord-like loch ringed by high mountains used as a 'deep harbour' by the Royal Navy fleet during both wars. With the breeze at my back, I got as close as I'll ever get to 'flying' down the western shore. When I turned northwards again, at the head of the loch, the wind almost brought me to a standstill. However, the views across to the northern cliffs of Ben Hope kept me pushing onwards. The forecast was for sunny intervals but these looked as if they would be measured in shutter speeds and Ben Hope was obviously reluctant to lose all of its cloud canopy.

Eventually, despite the wind, I reached the small village of Hope and detoured south along a minor road to reach the starting point of the walk up Ben Hope. This is a beautiful stretch of road following the shores of Loch Hope and passing through mixed woodland that cowers under the savage cliffs of the Ben. Although I had been hoping to climb the hill from the north and find a way through those cliffs, I chickened out because of the mist, instead making my way to the main footpath at the southern end of the loch. I did my best to hide the bicycle and then found the sign-posted route up the hill where the estate notice advises walkers to 'Kindly keep to the path'.

It was good to be walking with no heavy pack to carry. I was wearing trainers and, even worse, a white floppy sun hat. Clearly irresponsibly dressed for a hill walk, this, however, only occurred to me when I met a group of booted and balaclava-clad walkers emerging from the mist on their descent from the summit. They warned me about the cold winds. A little further on, I met some other climbers on their way down who looked me up and down before warning me about the cold winds and the poor visibility. As I neared the summit ridge, another couple making their way down warned me about the high winds, the poor visibility and the danger of walking over the cliffs. Perhaps they would have been just a little disappointed as they scanned the next day's papers to find no report of the mountain rescue of a sun-hat idiot. I had the summit to myself and cautiously explored the plunging northern cliffs, glad that I had had the sense to take the tourist route.

It was a slow cycle back up the eight miles to the village of Hope where I rejoined the main road to Tongue and started on the long uphill climb across the open moor of A' Mhòine. Tongue was still about twelve miles away and I was feeling very tired. Still, there was plenty of time to wonder just why I was putting myself through such pain to half-pedal, half-push my bike along the high and desolate road. I reached no firm conclusion before eventually getting to the top of the ridge near the isolated house at Moine, and from here, I began to view things differently – all the way down to the waters of the Kyle of Tongue. It was a relief to free-wheel down the cold, six-mile descent and watch the thin thread which stretched over the Kyle grow into the graceful curve of the causeway crossing over to the village of Tongue.

At the local Youth Hostel, I was so tired that I bought a tin of *chilli con carne* from the warden.

Whiten Head from the Coast road near Durness

Tongue to Stromness

I awoke to bright sunshine and the taste of *chilli con carne*. By seven o'clock, I was out enjoying the low morning sunlight which sharpened up the detail of the ridges on the northern rock faces of Ben Loyal. From the top of the road above Tongue, there was an even more impressive view of all the hills to the west, from Ben Hope to Foinaven, crouched along the northern edge of Scotland. A little further on, it looked as if the whole of northern Scotland was on view and at last I knew why I had resumed my journey. I reached the shore again at Bettyhill, a popular tourist village named after Elizabeth, Countess of Sutherland. The village itself was disappointing but the bay where the river Naver flows into the sea has a fine beach. Bettyhill seems an inappropriately jaunty name for a place so close to the savage Clearances of the past in nearby Strathnaver.

The road to Thurso keeps inland beyond Bettyhill only occasionally allowing glimpses of a wild coastline. As it was still a long way to Thurso, I resisted the chance to explore Strathy Point. A little further on, the road climbs up on to the headlands where the Orkney Islands appear as grey shapes in the blueness of the Pentland Firth. I hadn't realised just how close these islands are to the mainland. Mapmakers often use an inset or even a separate page for them when portraying the north of Britain, moving Orkney nearer to the Arctic Circle. I passed through Melvich, just a huddle of houses above the beautiful Melvich Bay, and down the steep hill to the Halladale River. Then it was uphill again, back onto the cliff-top road for even closer views across to Orkney. I also caught my first glimpse of the Dounreay Nuclear Power Station, a swollen dome like a boil on the landscape.

The road drops back down to sea level at the village of Reay and shortly afterwards passes through leafy woodland. On emerging from the wood, the rocky moor flattens out and transforms into cultivated farmland, more reminiscent of Norfolk than the Highlands.

I had now entered Caithness and had almost completed the crossing of Scotland's north coastline.

The Nuclear Power Station has transformed this part of Scotland, no doubt bringing much needed employment and finance. The wildness of the Sutherland hills is replaced by an airport runway and ploughed fields. There are shops at the roadside and traffic and then in a short time, the bustle of Thurso. Although I had planned to stay the night here, half an hour in those grey streets was long enough and I hurried off to the tourist office to find out about ferry crossings to Orkney. A ferry would leave Scrabster for Stromness at 5.45 p.m. I calculated that I had time to cycle eight miles to Dunnet Head, the most northerly point in Scotland, and back in time for the boat. Five miles from Thurso, I came across a signpost showing eight miles still to go! It was now three o'clock in the afternoon and commonsense would dictate that I had better abandon my attempt if I wanted to be sure of making the ferry. Instead, I kept on pedalling round the edge of Dunnet Bay and out to the Head.

Lighthouse at Dunnet Head and the Orkney Islands

It was worth all the rush to see those 300-feet-high red sea cliffs. There is a lighthouse perched on the edge and the clear views made Orkney appear close enough to touch. Even more impressive were the views along the whole length of Scotland's northern edge. To the east, some fifteen miles away, was Duncansby Head near John o' Groats and to the west were the distant cliffs of what I fondly believed to be Clò Mòr at Cape Wrath. It took me a long time to retrace those thirteen miles. By five o'clock, I was at last free-wheeling down to the slipway at Scrabster.

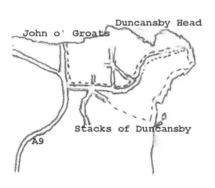

Seventy miles of hard cycling behind me, I lay down on a bench seat on the sea deck and fell fast asleep. When I woke up, the boat was nearing the island of Hoy and I joined the other passengers on the starboard side snapping photographs of the Old Man of Hoy – a sea stack of red sandstone which looked like a giant chess piece turning its regal back on the island's cliffs.

The Old Man of Hoy, Orkney

We docked at Stromness just after eight o'clock and even before I disembarked, I sensed a friendliness about the community. It was a grand place to start my first visit to Orkney, wandering along its narrow flagstone alleyways that run down to the water's edge. The occasional van racing past was a reminder that this was no pedestrian precinct: just narrow streets. A few of the shop windows had old-fashioned displays tainted with the shock of the new: 'Orkney Television Enterprise'. Having found a place to stay in a B&B overlooking the harbour, I went for a walk up the winding lanes to the top of the town which looked across the bay towards Hoy. So few people on the streets in broad daylight puzzled me. Surely they can't go to bed this early? I glanced at my watch to discover that it was a quarter to midnight. I hadn't appreciated just how far north I had come.

Skara Brae

Stromness to Kirkwall

A morning in Stromness was a gentle affair. The stone streets were slightly busier and the sea lapping at the waterfront more insistent than the previous night. Otherwise, there was little to disturb the still-life view over the town from the guest-house garden. An hour passed amongst the dahlias before I gathered up enough energy to head north on the main road to Skara Brae. Believing Orkney to be a barren place, the gentle landscape took me by surprise. I pedalled past fields of lush green grass where cows lay for a rest after a morning's munching and the hens ranged free. Scattered across the landscape were purposeful looking stones, some standing proud, some just leaning at ungainly angles, some in statuesque isolation and others just blocking up holes in the fence.

Although I had heard of the stone-age buildings at Skara Brae, I had no idea what they would look like. It took me slightly longer to reach them than expected and the first ancient dwelling house I spotted in the distance turned out to have a TV aerial on the roof. The settlement at Skara Brae, inhabited some 5,000 years ago when the Egyptians were building their pyramids, is impressively detailed. Transforming a low pile of stones into 'the palace storehouse' at archaeological sites can often require a vivid imagination. At Skara Brae, however, the walls are full height and practical installations such as beds and shelves can be clearly identified. Family life in this ageless village was not difficult to imagine and on the edge of the white sands and crystal clear waters of the curving Bay of Skaill, it was a good spot for a show house.

This was the most northerly part of my cycle, and rather than continuing round the mainland island, I headed south-east towards Stenness so that I could see that other great archaeological attraction. The Ring of Brodgar attracts coaches of tourists and when fully occupied, its wide circle of standing stones was slightly less mystical than I had hoped but still worth a quick circuit. Later, after only thirty miles cycling from Stromness, I pedalled in to Kirkwall, a busy town with a magnificent cathedral and some impressive storage tanks. The walls of St Magnus Cathedral glowed red in the afternoon sunshine and inside a dark blue haze disappeared into a calming gloom: a good place to sit listening to the sound of whispers and reflect on times past and future. Then it was off to the warmth of an excellent evening with Orcadian friends.

St Magnus Cathedral, Kirkwall

Kirkwall to Latheronwheel

J ust after nine o'clock, I left Kirkwall, fuelled by a good breakfast and a renewed enthusiasm only slightly dampened by a thick morning mist. Out past the Highland Park Distillery, I took the road heading south towards Burwick, some twenty miles away, where I was hoping to catch the late morning ferry back to the north coast of Scotland. Perhaps the slow pedalling was due to last night's sampling of 'You'll really like this malt.' Indeed, the Highland mist was real enough. It cleared briefly just as I reached the attractive little village of St Mary's at the southern coast of the mainland island. From here, the road crosses a series of causeways linking the islands of Burray and South Ronaldsay known as the Churchill Barriers. These narrow strips of land, built on massive concrete blocks, were constructed during the Second World War to protect the British fleet sheltering in Scapa Flow, the large bay ringed by Orkney's southern islands, from German U-boats. The sensation of cycling in the mist on the causeway through grey waters was very strange indeed. Even stranger were the large chunks of wrecks looming out of the foggy sea on either side, its waters looking rather like a ship stew.

'Ship Stew', Orkney

The first island reached is the small one of Lamb Holm, where Italian prisoners of war converted the interior of two Nissen huts into a brightly decorated chapel. I stopped and went inside. Despite its isolated position it is well maintained and freshly painted in bold colours. I reached Burwick at the southern end of South Ronaldsay in good time for the ferry where a small cabin at the pier offered shelter. Inside was another cyclist, a blonde-haired, super fit Dane dressed in shorts and T-shirt who seemed to be circling

Scotland in a long weekend. I retreated into my fleecy jacket and muttered something about hoping to reach Edinburgh by nightfall.

The Italian Chapel

It is only six and a half miles across the Pentland Firth to John o' Groats on mainland Scotland and a small passenger ferry makes the forty-five minute crossing several times a day during the summer months. The trip across a wild stretch of strong currents offers an exciting way to reach John o' Groats. Exhilaration evaporates fairly quickly, however, on arriving at the well-known extremity. Fortunately, I was just passing through. Had I travelled all the way from Land's End, I would have been sorely disappointed by a huddle of tourist buildings. I was relieved to escape quickly out of the village and head east along a minor road to Duncansby Head, the most north-easterly point on the British mainland. From the lighthouse high up on the cliffs, there are open views over the Pentland Firth and out across the cold gleam of the North Sea. I followed a track south along the edge of those sand-red cliffs, past cushions of sea pinks, and down towards the great sea stacks of Duncansby. These massive cones of rock appear to be floating at the water's edge and look as if they might set sail at any moment. This is a corner of Scotland to rival Cape Wrath and the rare chance to leave the tarmac for cliff-top tracks made the day's journey all the more worthwhile.

I returned to the main road to join the A9 on its long journey down south, beginning with the weary seventeen miles to Wick across the grey-brown moors of Caithness. There seemed to be so little colour here, the mist didn't help, and even the grass was a shade of fawn. Further south at Keiss, there is slightly more greenery but sadly little else to recommend the area. Even Wick, a place I hoped to declare much more attractive than I had expected, wasn't.

The sun came out, so did the wind and, as the coastline curved to the southwest, it was blowing straight towards me. The road was hard to travel with little scenic variety to take my mind off the wind. Then there were the high-sided trucks that roared their way south, sweeping me aside in their air stream. Becoming too tired for enjoyment, I was very relieved when I finally found a B&B in Latheronwheel and made my way to the local hotel for a meal. Inside, the barman was attempting to convince a customer that Pontius Pilate had been born in Perth: I was cheered by this piece of news. I thought he was from Edinburgh!

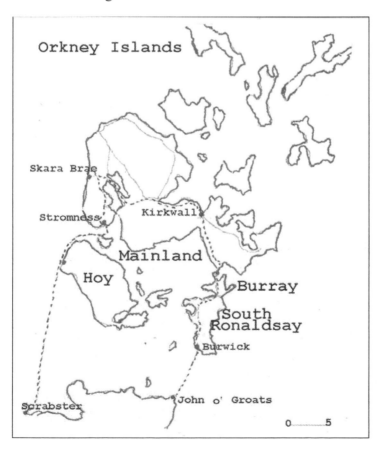

Latheronwheel to Tain

Another windy, grey-skied day. I was in some trepidation about today's cycle which would be a long one, travelling down the A9 along the eastern coastlines of Caithness and Sutherland. It is a hilly road, none more so than at Berriedale which nestles in the valley at the foot of the Berriedale Braes. The descent is long and steep and there is an even longer climb up the southern side. Still, the sun began to shine through the clouds, highlighting the green forest in the valley below and the patches of yellow whins on the headlands.

Helmsdale was built for the herring fishing boom in the last century. Nowadays, however, it looks as if it relies on teashops for wealth creation. They vie with each other to claim the most celebrated visitors. The great and the good have come here: well, Barbara Cartland anyway. I turned my back on the scones and headed on towards Brora where the landscape began to soften, giving wide views across rolling farmlands down to the Dornoch Firth. This is serious golfing country, last seen in Ayrshire, and there is a feeling of prosperity about the place now that the barren landscape of the north-east has been left behind. The photogenic towers and turrets of Dunrobin Castle, together with the surrounding gardens, are a reminder of the wealth of the Earls and Dukes of Sutherland and there is a large monument to the First Duke on the top of a nearby hill.

A minor road runs south of Golspie to Little Ferry. As I wasn't sure of the possibility of crossing the entrance to Loch Fleet by boat, I kept on the A9 inland and crossed the river on The Mound, a causeway built by Telford. The sun shone from a clear blue sky as I followed the road round the southern shore of Loch Fleet towards Embo and Dornoch. The road was flat, the sun warm and the sight of the hills to the north-west across the blue waters of the loch made the day's hard pedalling worthwhile. All was therefore well when I arrived in Dornoch. The Dornoch Castle Hotel was formerly the Bishop's Palace, which, together with the 13th century cathedral, forms the tranquil centre of this beautiful seaside town. The leafy gardens of the houses in the cathedral close, the sweep of white, sandy beach and one of the world's greatest golf courses make this an ideal place to stay for the night. So why did I decide to cycle on to Tain?

Dornoch

The Royal Burgh of Tain is a working town, lacking the elegance of Dornoch. It is, nevertheless, not short of an ancient building or two. A local tourist brochure describes the Tolbooth in the centre as 'massive and square and topped by fat candle-snuffer pinnacles, with a spire of similar shape'. This description hints at the impression left by the town, or perhaps I was just put off by the difficulty I had in finding anywhere to stay. I ended up in an extravagantly ornate red and black bedroom complete with cinema-curtain type net drapes.

Tain to Inverness

I was glad to escape those curtains into the early morning daylight across the flat farmlands south of Tain on my way to catch the first ferry of the day at Nigg. For the second time on my cycle journey, I was the sole passenger on a ferry. On this occasion, the small boat could have carried passengers and two cars across the Cromarty Firth to the town of Cromarty. The Nigg crossing has been in use since medieval times and is referred to as the King's Ferry, having been used by both King James IV and Robert the Bruce, on their way north to Tain. This short journey south takes a leap in time from the present day oil fabrication yards at Nigg and nearby Invergordon on the north coast of the Cromarty Firth, to the beautifully preserved 18th century town of Cromarty. Two hundred years ago, Cromarty was a bustling port and trading centre and many of the original buildings are still standing. The narrow streets and vennels lead past pebble-dashed cottages and the red sandstone grand houses of the merchants. Each turn of the corner has something different to offer, whether it is the Courthouse, built in 1763, the library gifted by Andrew Carnegie or the house of the geologist, Hugh Miller. There are cobbles and date stones, crow-stepped gables and, most important of all, the best doughnut of the journey so far.

The warmth of the morning sunshine brought out the scent of the broom blossom in the hedgerows as I cycled up the hill out of Cromarty and across the northern tip of the Black Isle. I followed the minor road from Newton that clings to the high ground, past Upper Cathie and Balmungie, stopping frequently to enjoy the views over to the snow-covered peak of Ben Wyvis in the east. Further on, the views across the Moray Firth began to open up and I saw, on the southern shore, The Bar: curves of sand that stretch out into the estuary near Nairn. The road then descends through a wooded 'Fairy Glen' and reaches the coast at Rosemarkie, a small but rather grand village of elegant red sandstone houses. I cycled past the links golf course to Chanonry Point, with the hope of catching a glimpse of the famous

bottlenose dolphins which live in the Firth. I contented myself instead
with a wander round the whitewashed lighthouse and the view of Fort
George across the water.

View across the Black Isle near Cromarty

I should have stopped to look at the ruined Cathedral at
Fortrose but as I was now getting tantalisingly near the week's
finishing point, I pressed on to Inverness instead. The road is forced
inland to circle Munlochy Bay and then I followed minor roads
through the Cacique Forest. The shopkeeper at Munlochy had warned
me that it was 'seven long miles to Kessock', and how right she was.
The nearer I got to the finish, the longer it seemed to take to get there.
With the puffed-up pride of a traveller, I crossed the Kessock Bridge
to make my entrance into the city of Inverness. Surprisingly few
people shared my sense of achievement, no one actually, but there was
little time for anticlimax as the next train to Edinburgh was leaving in
ten minutes. The only remaining problem was the dismantling of the
bike on the station platform and parcelling it up in poly bags because,
needless to say, there were no bicycle spaces available on the train. I

just made it, and collapsed into the only seat I could find. The young soldier in the next seat was keen to chat, showing some interest in my bright red sunburnt face. Perhaps he meant to be flattering when he said that he hoped that he would 'be as fit as you are when I'm your age.'

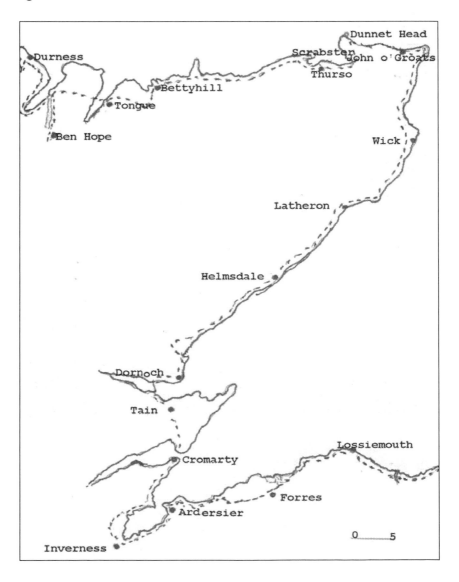

Part III

Knuckling Down

River Spey near Speybank

Inverness to Lossiemouth: 15 June 1996

Another June, another year and the sun was out in a clear sky when I left Inverness to follow the North-East Scotland Coastal Trail along the busy A96 road towards Nairn. At Newton, I turned off the main road north past Castle Stuart, the ancestral home of the Earls of Moray, to reach the coast just south of Ardersier. On the grassy track which runs along the side of the shingle beach, I stopped occasionally to take in the view across the Moray Firth to the hills in the west, and then on northwards to Fort George. This military fortress was built after Culloden to aid George the Second's subjugation of the Scottish Highlands and although impressive, some may disagree with the tourist brochure's claim that it is 'a must-see on any trip to the Highlands'.

That afternoon, the uprising continued as Scotland took on the 'Old Enemy' at Wembley in the knockout stage of the Europa 96 Cup. I listened to the first-half commentary on the radio, encouraged by the confident tone in the voices of the commentators as Scotland began to 'take control of the midfield' – it was just the ends now that they had to worry about! Nairn was indoors watching the televised match when I passed through and I didn't like to disturb it. So I cycled on and found a route into the great Culbin Forest, a nine-mile stretch of woodland bordering the coastal dunes. The maze of tracks through the forest seemed to lead nowhere in all directions, like a wood in Alice in Wonderland. There was no shortage of signs warning of the dangers of getting lost and endless rows of regimented pines gave little away. About a mile in, I took out my compass to check the direction for the sea. Even so, it took me some time before I eventually emerged from the trees into an open clearing amongst the rolling sand dunes.

In the middle of the clearing, some fifty yards away, a woman dressed in a white flowing dress stood motionless, bent double and staring closely at the ground. She was so still, as if posing for a picture – one of those weekend magazine elegant-model-in-deserted-landscape photographs. A few minutes later, she stood up and gracefully strolled up the shore leaving her well-crafted image behind her. Was she looking for gold coins from the smugglers' treasure which is supposed to lie buried in these sands of Culbin? Perhaps she was just waiting for someone to notice her, a photograph waiting to be taken. This whole area of coastline, once fertile and prosperous farmland, was flooded by sand during the great sandstorm of 1694. A contemporary account states that the storm arrived suddenly from the west one day in October. A high cloud of sand, some two miles wide, moved like a fast flowing river. The fields were submerged in a matter of hours and over the next few days, trees and houses were buried as hills of sand, up to a hundred feet high in places, formed. And if that wasn't bad enough, Scotland's missed penalty was followed by Gascoigne's goal.

I returned to the forest and cycled along deserted tracks through the tall pines for the next four miles, telling myself that I knew where I was going and keeping a watch out for capercaillies and Tweedledum. Neither had appeared by the time I reached Wellhill, (or was it the Lake of Moy?), where I left the woods and made my way on side roads to Forres. Here, the defeat at Wembley was being discussed in rhyming couplets by groups of supporters taking the air in the high street after enjoying some refreshment. The words 'English', 'shove' and 'up' provided the main theme for the chant. I took my English accent into Audrey's Tea Room, unsure whether I would be given the time to explain my Scottish ancestry. Mary Queen of Scots only spoke French when she returned to Scotland, so she presumably wasn't judged by her accent. The waitress was prepared to be tolerant of our southern friends – 'they can't help being English: they were born like it.' Yet, even she was slightly galled by the reaction of the elderly English couple who had been in earlier and apparently said 'Oh, bless them' when told that England had won. I don't think the two shopping-trolley-shoving supporters rolling along the main street were likely to bless anything this afternoon. I made a silent exit from Forres, pedalling wordlessly through the gathering crowds.

The seaside village of Findhorn was worth the detour, a cream-tea kind of place with white houses, marina people and early evening drinkers sitting outside the local pub. This is the third village of Findhorn; the previous two were drowned, first by sand and then by water. It is now surrounded by the neighbouring airbase and a craft village. I would have liked to stay but as accommodation was scarce, I retraced my route to Kinloss and headed east, past an uninviting looking Burghead, and on to Hopeman, only to find that all the B&B places were full. Surely a large place like Lossiemouth would have accommodation?

Findhorn

It was nearly nine o'clock when I finally made it to 'Lossie', cycling past the golf course and ducking involuntarily as a large helicopter flew over my shoulder. Apparently there was 'a big op' on at RAF Lossiemouth, or so all the full-guesthouse proprietors told me. By ten o'clock, it had come down to deciding between a hedgerow and a room at the Three Star Stotfield Hotel. Exhaustion must have impaired my judgement. I settled for the shelter of the poky room overlooking the kitchens at the back of the hotel. Perhaps there would be porridge and kippers for breakfast.

Lossiemouth to Pennan

Porridge and kippers were on the breakfast menu, along with orange juice with real bits in it, curled butter pats on a little dish, racks of toast and pots of tea. All was not wasted. In no hurry to leave the elegant, red-carpeted dining room, there was, nevertheless, a limit to the amount of toast I could eat: certainly not thirty-eight pounds worth. A thick sea haar was covering the town when I crossed the river Lossie and the eerie outline of an old railway bridge loomed out of the mist before disappearing into the sands of the estuary. Where was it taking people all those years ago?

A couple of miles from Lossiemouth, I turned off the road and entered another beautiful forest, following a grass-fringed track along corridors of dark pines. The mist cleared and the warmth of the day brought out the scent of the woodland, and ahead, a group of black rabbits partied on the path in the sunshine 'living on the wild side, close to the tracks, man'. This narrow stretch of forest follows the coast for about three miles, ending at the army rifle range at Bin Hill where I was able to return to the seashore to take the track along the edge of a shingle beach to the small village of Kingston on the shores of Spey Bay. There was once a great shipyard here using timber floated down the Spey from the Caledonian pine forests in the Cairngorms. I cycled inland across the field track to the stately little village of Garmouth, proud of its connection with Charles II who signed the Bill of Covenant here in 1650. In the village park, a group of children played a lacklustre game of football. No one today wants to be Gary McAllister. I took the cycle track east along a disused railway and sat down on one of the seats overlooking the golf course, watching some golfers chip away at disappointment. So much suffering on such a fine day!

The viaduct built by the Great North of Scotland Railway allows walkers and cyclists to cross the river Spey at this point whereas motorists have to detour south to reach the road bridge further inland. I was able to follow the Spey Way as it wound its way through the trees along the east bank before reaching the open sea at Tugnet where the vast banks of pebbles show how the power of this river continues to re-shape the surrounding area. I resisted the delights of the Ice House, the largest in Scotland, a 'must-see' for those interested in refrigeration, and continued cycling east instead, finding a route through yet another golf course onto a track by the beach.

Banks of pebbles at Spey Bay

I joined the coast road at Portgordon and pedalled on in the midday sun past Buckie, Findochty and Portknockie. There were brief glimpses from the road of towering cliffs and great knuckles of rock, some of them worn down by centuries of waves to form weird- shaped arches with names like the Bow Fiddle. Perhaps I should have spent more time exploring this stretch of the 'Grey Coast' but I was keen to keep cycling whilst the sun shone. I passed under the great viaduct at Cullen before stopping briefly at Portsoy to see some friends. Their cottage was silent and unresponsive, so, after a brief look at the stone harbour, it was on again to the busy ports of Banff and Macduff. I went into the local tourist office to book some B&B accommodation at a farmhouse in Pennan and the woman behind the counter gave me a booking form which asked me to state the 'Starting point of journey'. 'Just put England' she said conclusively. Perhaps it was just as well I had taken shelter in Audrey's tearoom yesterday.

Coastline near Portknockie

The shore, guarded by high cliffs for the next few miles, forced me and the main road inland for a hot pedal over the headland before reaching the turn-off for Gardenstown. This narrow side road plunges down through a gap in the cliffs, passing the Chapel of Skulls where the heads of killed Scandinavian invaders used to be displayed as wall ornaments. Deciding not to stop, I weaved my way through the tightly-packed houses that cling to the terraces of Gardenstown, a village built on the side of the cliffs. The sound of hymns sung by Methodists greeted me as I sped past a church building; but there again it could have been the voices of the Brethren, Plymouth or Open, the Salvation Army, the Baptists (Strict or Particular) or even

Papists. It is a broad church in 'Gamrie' (the name locals use) with a religion for everyone – one each. On a dark cold Sunday in winter, this village will squeeze the irreverent breath out of you but on this sunny Sunday afternoon, even the wind seemed relaxed. The backdrop of the cliffs which tower above the small fishing village was reflected in the mirrored surface of the harbour waters as I sat on the sea wall to bask in the calm of the scene.

   At the east end of the harbour, there is a narrow track, hewn out of the base of the cliffs, round the rocky headland to the next fishing village of Crovie. I had been looking forward to cycling this mile of coast, within spraying distance of the sea, and which has magnificent views across the bay to the neat white line of houses huddled below the red cliffs at Crovie. In his book *One Foot in the Sea,* Robert Smith describes Crovie as keeping 'a fragile hold on the land' and when you see the single row of fisherman's cottages, the gable ends almost dipping into the sea, his words are easily understood. In fact, the great storm of 1953 forced most villagers to move out onto the higher and safer slopes of Gardenstown.

The village of Crovie

It was a long and hard push up from Crovie, a one in five gradient (so the sign says), to reach the top of the headland and the main road again. I was heading for Pennan, wearying my way over the last few hilly miles of the day to reach my pre-booked B&B which turned out to be several miles south of the village. Then, after a brief rest, I was back out again to cycle those same hills back to Pennan – all for a chance to see my 'Local Hero' for a pint. It had taken me two years to cross from the dining room to the bar of this film set, all the way from Lochailort to Pennan. It was worth the wait. The village itself, tucked into a narrow cleft in the cliffs, seemed pleasantly familiar even though the photogenic red telephone box was in the wrong place. I sat down at one of the tables next to the harbour and, as the sun disappeared behind a layering of clouds, I began to sense that this was a secretive place and could understand why it used to earn more from smuggling than fishing. Then, from beneath those grey clouds over the northern headland, a trace of pink appeared in the sky. A bulging blood-red sun descended gently through a gap in the lower cloud and the windows of Pennan turned crimson for a few admirable minutes before disappearing from view for a second time. Was this a real sunset on the east coast or mere trick photography?

Pennan to Aberdeen

The wind had blown up during the night and I was tired after yesterday's ten and a half hours of pedalling. The day's planned journey round the 'knuckle of Scotland' would also be hard work and I started out pedalling in earnest, despite the huge farmhouse breakfast – served with 'pork sausages in case you're worried about this BSE disease scare'. I think that the landlady was making a point about the stupidity of such a belief rather than wanting to reassure me! The wind was happily blowing from the west, and in a relatively short time, I was cycling into Fraserburgh underneath a great flock of gulls swarming like large white flies over the waste bins of the fish processing plant on the edge of town. Fraserburgh appeared to be closed and shuttered, perhaps one of the reasons for the old man in the High Street raging at passers-by. He stood alone on the pavement and shook his fists at the sky. I think that I might have ended up joining him if I were to stay here too long.

Apart from a brief detour to visit the silent village and beach of St Combs, I kept to the country roads, away from the coast, and reached 'The Blue Toon' of Peterhead by midday. The school children were out for lunch and the place had a more cheerful liveliness about it than I had expected. I cycled down to the harbour in search of Scotland's most easterly point on the mainland. A security man in the adjoining oil-rig yard asked me why I was trespassing on his reclaimed land tip which forms this corner of Scotland. He laughed when I explained my mission, wondering why someone would be so daft as to want to visit the waste ground. No, he doubted if a celebratory plaque was likely to be erected but he admitted that I wasn't the first to visit – some writer had been before and mentioned it in his book. And that is how rumours start.

The lighthouse on Buchan Ness, previously the most easterly point before the harbour extension, is reached by a bridge across the North Sea and is a much more impressive extremity. I circled this tiny island and then crossed back to join the main road south, stopping briefly to look at the Bullers of Buchan where the headland has made a spectacular collapse into the sea. Great gashes in the ground separate narrow ridges of red granite cliffs that plunge to the waters hundreds of feet below. Tired legs and the gusting wind dissuaded me from following the feint paths along the knife-edged crests – it must be a nightmare of a place to visit with children. A few miles further on, I left the road and followed a short track across the headland to the cliff-top ruins of Slains Castle, claimed by some to be the inspiration of another nightmare, Count Dracula. Several groups of tourists were clambering over the ruined walls and some Americans asked if I knew where to find the 'sugar-loaf – you know, where the young boy was killed'. For some reason, I was pleased that I didn't know, and left them to their macabre search amongst the ruins of this cardboard cut-out-looking castle. Beyond the castle, the track led south across the top of the headland before dipping down to a gorge and then through an orchard of trees into the village of Cruden Bay.

Slains Castle, near Cruden Bay

Once described as the Brighton of Aberdeenshire, Cruden Bay has had a long history as a tourist centre and had a fleet of electric

trams in its heyday. The Cruden Bay Hotel was built by the Great
North Railway to accommodate millionaires, including the barons of
food processing such as Mr Colman of mustard and the ovenly
Crawfords. The Gilbeys and the Wills came, as did Burrell and, of
course, Bram Stoker, the author of Dracula, all to enjoy a magnificent
beach and golf. But they hadn't been looking for a B&B. It was now
late afternoon and, after forty miles of cycling, I was ready to stop for
the day and enjoy this tourist Mecca. There appeared to be only one
guesthouse in town and the owner was obviously unimpressed by my
singular request for a room. The two hotels I tried were also full and I
began to feel even more tired at the prospect of pedalling several miles
to the next village. I bought a fish supper to take in some fuel and
asked the owner whether he knew of any places to stay. Perhaps chip
shop conversations are sometimes difficult to follow but it was the
man's dialect that defeated me. Never having had a problem
understanding Scottish accents, on this occasion the thick
Aberdeenshire one was beyond me. I think he asked if I had tried
'Dougal's'.

  'Is that Dougal's?' I asked.
  'No, Donan's', he replied.
  'Ah Donan's, yes?' I said confidently.
  'No, Donald's'
  'Right, so that's Donald's?' I asked rather tentatively.
  'No, Dougal's' he said emphatically.
  'Ah, yes, well thanks, that's been very useful.' I said smiling.
  I hid from the wind behind a bank on the golf course, ate my
fish meal, and felt more enthusiastic about leaving Cruden Bay.
  When the road out of town was uphill and into the wind, self-
pity set in again. In the next village, Newburgh, ten miles away,
nobòdy was very hopeful of any accommodation being available there
either, unless of course Dougal Donan lived there. The road turned
south about a mile further on and the wind returned, this time at my
back. Now the pedals turned more easily and I began to enjoy myself
again. Surely I could manage another nine miles?

I kept to the main A975 road and ignored signs to the interesting cliff-top villages of Whinnyfold and Collieston which had been on my planned route. There was no obvious place to stay in Newburgh, not that I looked too hard because I was tempted by the green road sign which indicated that Aberdeen was only thirteen miles away. For some reason my feebleness at Cruden Bay had now been replaced by a greedy desire to get in the miles. The wind was still at my back and sweeping through the green fields of swaying barley at the roadside, as I moved onto busier roads and pedalled with even more determination. Perhaps it was that fish supper?

Big roads mean big trucks and bikes don't fare too well in the down-draught of a juggernaut. I was almost swept off my bike on several occasions on the A92 trunk road into Aberdeen. It was now just after nine o'clock in the evening and the closer I got to Aberdeen, the wearier I felt. The nearer I come to a planned stop, the greater the exhaustion. If I am forced to continue beyond my original destination, my mind automatically re-tunes my level of tiredness, only to repeat the process at the next planned stopping place. All rather feeble really, but I was very glad to see the B&Q sign on the outskirts of Aberdeen. It confirmed that I had reached the city, because, like the rest of us, Aberdonians won't travel too far out of the centre for the wallpaper paste. I felt a real sense of achievement as I entered this great city after seventy miles of pedalling. I certainly felt more deserving of a sense of arrival than the drivers of the cars and trucks that queued up alongside me at the traffic lights. I had really been on the road.

Finding a place to stay was certainly easy enough, although I turned down the first Guest House which was charging thirty-five pounds for bed, breakfast and 'thirty television channels'. I found another nearby, a mere four-channel one, charging a paltry twenty-five pounds. Television must be very expensive in Aberdeen! I went down to Bond's Bar for a pint of beer. It was crowded with students and young blades who drank beer from the neck of the bottle. I kept hoping that the guitarist would play some early Dylan but the closest he got was 'American Pie'. I felt tired and rather old, particularly when the students at the next table bemoaned the passing of their empty youth: 'God, Jessica's twenty-six and she's already married and everything, and I'm just … ' I was too tired for four, let alone thirty channels when I arrived back to the guest house.

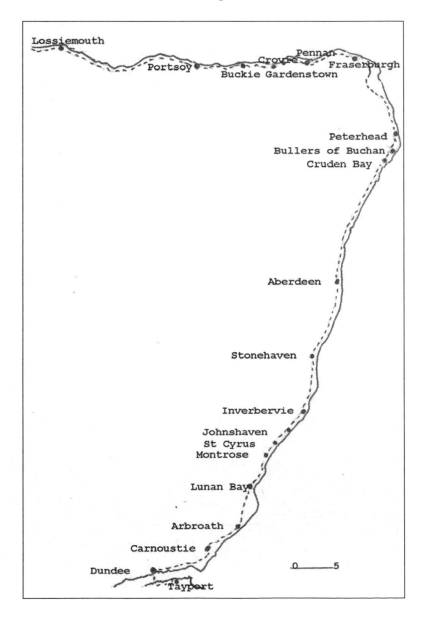

Aberdeen to Lunan Bay

Aberdeen's city-centre buildings looked crisp, clean and business-like, gleaming with granite and self-importance, as I made my way down to the harbour and looked back across the boats to a great city skyline of towers and spires. Like Dundee and Liverpool, Aberdeen doesn't hide its port and brings its ships, with exotic names like 'Sun Wrestler', almost into the High Street. London and Edinburgh are just realising now that shipping can be seen as well as heard. As there was much to see in this city, I decided to ignore all of it rather than just some and embarked on the slow pedal uphill on the road south instead. Nevertheless, having gone along to Bond's Bar, I could proudly claim to have seen more of the city than Jonathan Raban did on his sail round the British coast.

The harbour at Aberdeen

In his book *Coasting,* Raban describes how a thick sea mist forced him to steer clear of the Aberdeen harbour shipping traffic and his only reported memory of the place were the sights, sounds and smell of this great city's sewage outlet. Another coastal traveller and comparative literary giant, Paul Theroux, who at least stayed one night in Aberdeen, was equally unimpressed; in fact he 'came to hate Aberdeen more than any place I saw'. Mind you, his book about his journey around the coast of Britain, *The Kingdom by the Sea,* doesn't convey much enthusiasm for many of the places he visited. His view of Scotland was largely from a railway carriage, missing out some of the best parts of the west coast from Lochalsh to Durness. He was, though, very impressed by Cape Wrath, describing it as one of the few places in the world where travellers might sense that they were 'discovering' it for the first time. Jonathan Raban, on the other hand, missed out the whole of the north coast of Scotland altogether, ducking down the Caledonian Canal to save time. I would like to have caught sight of them, a brief wave would have been enough. They did meet up with each other on their travels, near the nudist beach in Brighton. Both refer to the beach in their accounts of their brief lunch meeting, claiming that they were not spending a lot of time writing up notes. Otherwise, there is little similarity about their book entries and about as much warmth between them as presumably a Brighton nudist feels. It was just as well that they had chosen to travel round the coast in opposite directions. Oh, and yes, Paul did find time to say how much he hated Brighton.

Back to tarmac, the sun moved through layers of grey cloud and the main road stretched into the distance. I was now cycling up onto the headlands, away from the coast, with only brief glimpses of the steely waters of the North Sea. Thanks to a following wind, I was in high gears and spirits, covering the fifteen miles to Stonehaven in less than an hour. Splashes of sunlight lit up the farmlands, bringing out the rich colours of a bedspread of a landscape – acres of yellow rape flowers, furrows of red soil and fields of green barley. I had cycled this road once before, in the opposite direction, but as it was thirty-five years ago, I could remember little about the countryside. A friend and I had sailed up to Dundee from London on board a Dundee, Perth and London Shipping Company coaster and made our way to Aberdeen. This, therefore, was a nostalgic journey, spoilt only by the almost constant threat of decapitation from passing lorries. Truck drivers seemed to think that they could sway by without moving off their line for a mere cyclist on the inside lane. But tarpaulin is an acquired taste and on several occasions I began to wonder whether I was very near to, or just under the enormous wheels of these raging wagons. Unfortunately, the handlebars were shuddering too much to risk releasing a fist to shake at their distant taillights. I shouted abuse instead, safe in the knowledge that if, by any remote chance they could actually hear my oaths, it would take them until Montrose before they could slow down sufficiently to stop and respond in some jocular fashion to my puny quips.

Dunnottar Castle

From the village of Muchalls, the main road and railway line cling to the coastal cliffs and there are distant views over to the houses of Stonehaven huddled round the harbour. From this ancient burgh, I followed the narrow road which circles the cliffs on the south side of town and cycled along the track over the headland to the ruined castle of Dunnottar. Used by Zeffirelli as a location for his film of Hamlet and by the locals to hide the Scottish crown jewels from Cromwell, this sinister but very photogenic fortress is perched on a circle of crags with the crater of ruined walls seemingly growing out of the rock.

I ignored the side road to the village of Catterline and kept on the main road south through an atmospheric landscape of open farmlands as dark shadows of cloud swept across the vast fields of corn. I later found out that I was looking across the Howe of Mearns and the area known as Arbuthnott which Lewis Grassic Gibbon used as his setting for *Sunset Song*. He cycled along these roads on a bike he called his 'clank and groul'. Mine was more of a screech and judder at that moment.

At Inverbervie, I was at last able to leave the A92 and find a stretch of off-road cycling by following an old track known as the Low Road which runs along the edge of the shingle beach. It is an untidy foreshore where the wrecks of old cars and other debris from land meets the flotsam of the sea. This tired-looking road, overgrown in places, connects a string of silent and deserted fishing villages and there is a general feeling of neglect and dereliction about the area. Although more heavily populated than the west coast, many parts of the eastern edge seem very lonely and isolated. Perhaps this is due to the emptiness of the view across the North Sea compared with the companionship of the islands in the west. The local fishing industry has all but disappeared, along with the whole of Miltonhaven, a village which was swept into the sea two centuries ago. The track ends just north of Tangleha, 'Seaweed Haven', one of the strange sounding names in the area along with Horse Creek Bay and Sillyflatt. I returned to the tarmac for the next two miles to St Cyrus, a small village at the north end of a beautiful stretch of sand which curves round Montrose Bay. Hoping to cycle along the beach, I was deterred by the prominent 'No Cycling' sign and had to settle instead for the view from the cliff top of the pale sands and the delicate lattice work of salmon fishermen's nets built along the water's edge.

The beach at St Cyrus

Montrose has an old-fashioned air about it and appeared to have changed little since my last visit as a child to see my grandfather. Now I had my own generation of relatives to meet and I stopped for a very pleasant couple of hours at my cousin's house. The waters of the Montrose Basin were gleaming in the early evening sunshine as I crossed the bridge over the South Esk and climbed uphill towards Braehead. Then I took the back roads to Lunan Bay and found a place to stay in an elegant lodge house at the end of a long crunchy gravel drive surrounded by freshly mown lawns.

Lunan Bay to Anstruther

The elegant dining room was darkly furnished and the gloom of the old-fashioned decor was lit from the narrow gap in the shuttered windows and by the yellow gleam of a vast slab of smoked haddock which lay across my breakfast plate. It was a reckless decision to agree to take two pieces of haddock after porridge

and I regretted it as soon as the words were out of my mouth. There was no going back: the haddocks and I had the room to ourselves and we ate or were eaten in respectful silence until we were all exhausted.

Arbroath Abbey

I cycled down to the small village of Lunan and walked across the sands of its beautiful bay. The tide was out and it was very peaceful to watch the low, rolling waves lap gently over the red sands. My sense of calm was soon left at the water's edge as I hurried along the narrow back roads through Redcastle and Auchmithie to Arbroath. Patches of blue sky appeared, lighting up the distant hills and glens of Angus and by the time I reached Arbroath, the red sandstone of the ruined abbey was glowing in bright sunshine. It was nearly lunchtime and the town was shopping-busy and noisy with traffic. Too much traffic to cope with the narrow streets led to a road being built right through one of the arches of the historic abbey.

Here we have an early example of traffic management in the town where the Scottish Declaration of Independence was signed in 1320.

I left Arbroath on the main A92 Dundee road. Six miles on, I escaped from the heavy lorries to follow a side road down to Carnoustie on the coast. The town's famous golf course was busy and I sat for a time comparing the upright confident posture of those about to drive off the first tee with the wearied droop of those struggling onto the eighteenth green. I, also, began to droop on the long seven-mile cycle from Monifieth to the centre of Dundee. The sun almost always seems to shine on this much-maligned city and the Tay does look silvery particularly if you see it from high up on the west side. I visited Balgay above the Perth road and then dropped down to the Tay Road Bridge. Cyclists and pedestrians have been given pride of place on a centre lane all to themselves and I took my time crossing, enjoying the wide-open views upstream past the low railway bridge and eastwards out to the open sea.

Once across the bridge, I headed east towards Tayport where I visited several cul-de-sacs before finding the route into the Tentsmuir Forest. There is a network of well-surfaced tracks through the forest and to avoid getting lost I followed the one closest to the edge and kept sight of the Abertay Sands which stretch some five miles out to sea beyond the trees. The warm early evening sunshine brought out the scent of the pines and at the south-easterly corner of the forest, I stopped to have a walk through the high sand dunes.

I left the southern end of the forest and pedalled along a rather grand sunlit avenue of tall beech trees before emerging into the open countryside near the village of Leuchars. Neat houses with manicured lawns and flower-filled gardens surrounded an impressively buttressed Norman church, a kind of miniature Notre Dame, and just over the honeysuckle hedge, a large jumbo jet taxied down the runway. The scent of garden blossom mingled with the heady aroma of aircraft engine fuel from the neighbouring RAF station. Still, it is a very pretty village.

St Andrews' tailored greenery and crown of spires looked as elegant as usual. Mary Queen of Scots reputedly considered St

Andrews as the finest town in her kingdom, but there again, she was a golfer! Stopping here for the night was out of the question. The town's accommodation was full as new graduates promenaded with their families to celebrate academic success. I felt out of place amongst the gowns and 'No Vacancy' signs and left to make my way round the East Neuk of Fife. While there is a coastal path for walkers along the coastline, cyclists have to take to the main road – another ten miles for me in the evening sunshine. As the university family celebrations had swept up all the accommodation in the pretty seaside village of Crail, it was half-past-nine at night before I eventually found a B&B in the neighbouring fishing village of Anstruther.

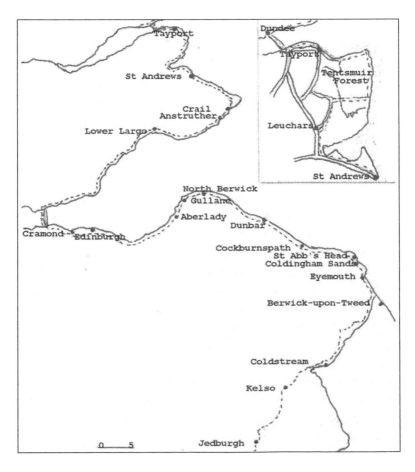

Anstruther to Edinburgh

The all-pervading sense of anti-climax which had characterised the week's cycling was still with me as I left to follow a section of the coastal path around the edge of Anstruther's golf course to the next fishing port of Pittenweem. Although these are pleasant places to visit, as were many of the other towns and villages seen that week, there had been too much time spent on tarmac and often a long day's cycling stretching far into the evening in search of somewhere to stay. Endurance and mileage sometimes had become more important than the simple pleasure of being out on the open road and I was looking forward to being home again.

A 'No Cycling' sign marking the next section of the coastal path to St Monans meant that it was back to the main road again for the journey to the prosperous village of Elie. About a mile and a half outside this attractive village near Kilconquhar Loch, an unmarked side road on the left follows the disused railway line along the coast for several miles to Lower Largo. The road, soon becoming a track crossing farmlands, was still a good enough surface to cycle on and worth the effort for the views south across Largo Bay and the Firth of Forth. Lower Largo is the birthplace of Alexander Selkirk, the original desert islander, and I spent some time walking up and down the main street looking for the Robinson Crusoe statue before I discovered it peering down at me from above a doorway.

The co-authors of *Walking Britain's Coast* provide a very comprehensive and detailed description of Scottish shores. On reaching this point on the coastline, they respectfully advise walkers to take a bus from Leven to Kirkcaldy and that the train which 'hugs the coast' to the Forth Bridge offers an attractive alternative to walking. Now there's tact for you! I pedalled on, not lingering on the way to Aberdour except to wonder briefly why so many people had decided to perch caravans on the cliffs at Burntisland. In contrast, Aberdour has a discreet charm about it. The village is tucked into a rocky corner of the coast overlooking the island of Inchcolm, a mile out in the Firth of Forth across a stretch of water known, for some reason, as Mortimer's Deep. The railway station, bedecked with hanging baskets of flowers grown by the stationmaster, had been famous for some time. I followed the main road round to Inverkeithing and cycled across the Forth Road Bridge. Although it is not as impressive looking as its neighbouring rail bridge, it offers two miles of very exciting cycling, particularly when the cross winds blow. The side lane for cyclists and pedestrians is at the very edge of the bridge and, as the whole suspended structure shakes with the rumble of passing heavy vehicles, there seems to be very little metal between you and the waters of the Forth some hundred feet below.

I took the back road down the steep hill to South Queensferry. From the east end of the village, there is a fine walk along the foreshore to Hound Point and along estate tracks past Barnbougle Castle to a small passenger ferry which will take walkers across the River Almond to the village of Cramond. Unfortunately, as cyclists are not welcome on the estate, I had to take the main road to Cramond Brig and then cross the bridge to follow the riverside track along the east bank of the river Almond down to Cramond. The waters are dark and still on this upper stretch of river above the weir, banks overgrown with giant mallows, deep green scrambling bushes and weeping trees. When the track narrows to a path about half way along as the cliffs crowd the water's edge, I had to carry the bike up and over a wooden staircase. This proved truly worth the effort to reach Cramond Village, its harbour, in use since Roman times, and a terraced bank of whitewashed houses. Then it was off, past the causeway to Cramond Island and along to the promenade at Silverknowes. Another mile, and I had reached my house in north Edinburgh, glad of a rest after the week's three hundred miles of pedalling. I was looking forward to that curry.

Part IV

Crossing the Borders

Mary Queen of Scots' house, Jedburgh

Edinburgh to Coldingham Sands: 7 June 1997

Until recently, Edinburgh had turned its back on the coastline. Few visitors to the Edinburgh Festival would head as far north as Newhaven or even Portobello. Some years ago, however, Leith led the way in bijou-ing the strip of shore between the gas works at Granton and the sewage stream at Seafield. Now there is even talk of marinas and waterfront hotels; Granton might yet be restored to the former glory of the time when the first train ferry in the world sailed between Granton and Fife.

From this north side of the city, I started out to meet a friend at Portobello on my last week of coastal journeying. Portobello is the only part of 'Edinburgh-on-Sea' with a fine stretch of sandy beach. The long promenade seafront made for a pleasant early morning cycle as the promenaders had not arrived yet: just a few stray dogs and fierce looking joggers. After Joppa, we had to cycle on the main A199 for half a mile or so before turning off, past the little harbour at Fisherrow, to cross the pedestrian bridge over the river Esk at Musselburgh. A left turn along the east bank of the river took us to the back straight of the town's racecourse and a mile of cycling along the grass track close to the rails. The wind was at our back and the going was good to soft. We then followed the sign-posted cycle route to Prestonpans and found our way onto a route at the back of the town, down to the harbour and along the top of the sea wall.

The surface on the concrete wall was roughly pitted and flooded in parts. Some less experienced cyclists might even have considered it dangerous. However, after a thousand miles of crossing all kinds of rock and tarmac, I was a good judge of whether ground was safe to cycle on. Even whilst I was crashing down, taking a closer look at the concrete, I was still feeling confident. I felt less so when my body hit the green slime. More upsetting was the fact that Alastair had somehow managed to stay on his feet despite me kicking his bike from under him as I fell. I muttered something about lichen lichens and did my best to save face, claiming that my aching knee only required a cursory flick. After all those miles on my own, I had to wait until I had half an hour of company before falling off my bike!

A track led down to the power station at Cockenzie and then we re-joined the main road, passing the rocky shores of Seton and Gosforth Sands before disappearing into the woods on the way to Aberlady. The coast is reached again at Aberlady Bay and we were able to leave the tarmac and follow the track into the nature reserve around Gullane Point. Having crossed the wooden bridge, we examined the swathe of notices for any 'No Cycling' signs. Finding none, we made our way along the grassy track around Gullane Links, crossing deserted golf course fairways before reaching the Hummell Rocks at the start of Gullane Bay. Despite Edinburgh being still in view back along the Forth, there is a remoteness about Gullane Point, appreciated perhaps by the thousands of geese and other birds that spend the winter nesting on this part of the coast.

As the tracks softened into the sandy dunes, it became impossible to cycle. We pushed our way to the top of Gullane Bents to view the sweep of sands in Gullane Bay. Although it would have been good to continue along the beach to North Berwick, it was hard work trying to cycle across soft sand. Instead, we made our way into the village of Gullane. Staying on the main A198 road for only about a mile, we found a route (marked 'Private' but recommended by a local as his shortcut back from the pub) along an estate track near Archerfield which took us to Dirleton. It is an attractive village with a handful of houses clustered round the pub and village green and could almost be Ambridge. Phil Archer, however, has never mentioned anything about a ruined castle! In another two miles, we had reached North Berwick, having covered over two-thirds of the last twenty-five miles from Edinburgh on off-road cycling.

The main road south from North Berwick climbs up onto the top of the headlands. It was hard work, especially since I couldn't get off and walk, not with Alastair clinging to my back wheel poised for a break. So it was a breathless competitive pedal, past the curtain wall of Tantallon Castle and along a minor road to Seacliff. It took us some time to find our way through the network of farm roads to Scoughall. In truth, I got lost! But it was a peaceful cycle, whirring quietly along between fields of green barley. Looking left at one point, I was surprised to see a great white mound of rock rising up out of the fields and it took me a few seconds to realise that this was the Bass Rock, a volcanic island whitened by colonies of birds. When I eventually gave up trying to find a way along the coast to Tyninghame House, it was back to the main road, past the old church at Whitekirk and downhill to the village of Tyninghame.

Alastair left to race back to Edinburgh and I followed the track at Kirklandhill through clusters of tall pines, around the edge of the beautiful John Muir Country Park to West Barns on the outskirts of Dunbar. Because of some serious digging beyond Dunbar, I couldn't see any alternative but to miss out Torness Point to join the traffic on the A1 trunk road. It was a hard cycle, battling between a head wind and the sideways draught of international lorries swishing their way south past the billowing clouds emerging from the cement works and along to Torness Nuclear Power Station before escaping at Cockburnspath. I took the narrow side road that winds steeply down to Pease Bay and stopped for some late lunch to enjoy the view across fields of rape and barley to the red cliffs circling the bay. This is a beautiful stretch of shore on the east coast, particularly if you are travelling by bicycle or inter-city train. I was warming to my week of cycling.

I must have appeared sufficiently familiar with my surroundings for a passing motorist to ask me whether it was a through road. I certainly hoped so because it seemed a long way down to the caravans at Pease Bay and once there, the only way forward was up again, climbing all the way to Woodend on the Coldingham road. It was hard work getting to the top of the headland at Haud Yauds and I stopped to look at the view across Pease Bay and out to the open sea. Edinburgh already seemed a very long way away.

Maps had indicated that a route across Telegraph Hill and along the cliff tops to St Abb's Head might be possible from Haud Yauds. I settled instead for five miles of free-wheeling down the main road to Coldingham. I was glad to have booked a bed for the night in the Youth Hostel, my first night in one since Tongue. The hostel at Coldingham Sands is an impressive mansion perched on the headland. Only a green lawn away from the top of the cliffs, it reminded me of the 'Camomile Lawn' television series. There was no sign of anyone when I pushed open the porch door. Some residents then began to appear along the narrow cliff-top paths. The warden appeared from nowhere to tell me that there was no bed available unless I wished to share with nine school children. For some reason I declined and found a room in the neighbouring St Veda's House, a small guest house

overlooking a quiet, sandy cove. It had been a long sixty miles from Edinburgh and it was good just to laze on the double bed after a shower, enjoying the view, of the beach framed in the window. One moment it was summer, full of children playing and grown-ups strolling at the water's edge: the next minute, winter, empty, as a thunderstorm passed overhead.

Beach theatre at Coldingham Sands

Indoors, on the television, Fred Trueman was extolling the virtues of the Australian cricket captain's gritty century – 'after all the criticism he's received from the press and former players'. As a former player and member of the press, thank goodness we can rely on your ever-present generosity of spirit.

Once the storm had passed over, I set off to cycle along the cliff-top path, north of Coldingham Sands, to the small fishing village of St Abbs and walked the two miles along the cliffs to St Abb's Head. The place is said to be named after St Ebba, a Northumbrian Princess, who was shipwrecked whilst escaping from the King of Mercia. This is a coastline to rival Ardnamurchan Point, and certainly one of the most impressive spots on the east coast of Scotland. It was some time before I turned my back on those rugged cliffs for a pint in the Anchor Inn.

The cliffs and village of St Abbs

Coldingham Sands to Kelso

At breakfast in the small dining room, the bearded violinist sitting behind me told me all about bee keeping and I also overheard that the baby with the couple at the other table had 'smallpox; no I mean chicken pox!' This is a busy time of year for beekeepers, keeping an eye on the queen bee in case she starts to act strangely and fly off somewhere. If she goes, then the rest follow and once out of sight, the bees are no longer the property of the beekeeper. Apparently, the law defines bees as domestic animals whilst they are kept within sight of the keeper's property. If, however, the swarm disappears, they are considered to be wild and can be captured by a neighbour who might have been secretly waiting years for just this opportunity. That would explain why the guesthouse owner in Latheronwheel told me that her husband was out stalking his queen bee. And I had felt so sorry for her. The lady of the house that is.

Boats at Eyemouth

The coastal path to Eyemouth, I was told, wasn't suitable for cycling, so it was back through Coldingham village, stopping briefly to hear the orchestra rehearsing in the local hall, and onto the A1107. Eyemouth looks as if it has known busier days than this leisure-filled Sunday. While a party of divers made their way out to sea in a small inflatable dingy, all the large fishing boats were tied up on the far side of the harbour, looking very smart and important. I made my way back uphill out of the town, following a side road to Burnmouth, before joining the traffic on the A1 for the last few miles to the English border at Lamberton.

I had spent several winter evenings trying to decide which route I should take to cross back to the west coast. I had thought about cycling the Southern Upland Way from Cockburnspath to Portpatrick, but that route would have missed out St Abb's Head and the Solway Coast. I opted instead to cross the country as close to the border as possible, initially following the River Tweed before crossing the Cheviot Hills to Liddesdale and Gretna.

The A1 and the railway line run side-by-side along the top of the cliffs all the way to the Border which appeared sooner than I expected and was marked by a rather discreet rectangular stone engraved with a shield and 'England'. In contrast, the 'Welcome to Scotland' sign on the other side of the road was big, blue and made of girders. The low stonewall next to the English stone had been partially demolished, perhaps as part of some symbolic gesture, although the collapsed part of the wall had fallen onto the Scottish side. Was this the English breaking out?

I turned off the A1 and headed up a narrow side road to the viewpoint near Camphill. To the south, the English coastline stretched out beyond Berwick-Upon-Tweed and I could just see Bamburgh Castle far in the distance. One of these days, I thought, I'll spend some time in Berwick-Upon-Tweed – longer than my only other visit to date when I had become trapped behind the doors of an inter-city train in Edinburgh's Waverley Station. It had been an unexpected outing, particularly as I had been only seeing some friends onto the train, when the automatic doors clicked shut and it was 'Next stop Berwick'.

This can be awkward when you've left your car on a double yellow line and told your family that you would be back in half an hour! Even though I had to wait over an hour on Berwick Station for a north-bound train, I was too busy swearing and composing my letter to British Rail to savour the delights of the royal burgh.

Dusk on the River Tweed

The River Tweed forms the border between Scotland and England from just outside Paxton to Coldstream and I followed a route along the minor roads which make up a section of the Tweed Cycleway. I stopped at Ladykirk to look inside the small stone-roofed church, The Kirk of Our Lady of the Steill. The muscular buttressed walls seemed somewhat out of place in these quiet farmlands. According to legend, King James IV of Scotland was nearly drowned crossing the nearby ford and vowed to build a church in memory of the Blessed Virgin of the Steill who had saved him. The church leaflet explained that his vow specified that the church should be one that could not be destroyed by either fire or flood – quite significant at a time of cross-border raids and frequent flooding of the Tweed valley. Here was, for me, the first indication of the turbulent history of this seemingly tranquil countryside. A mile later, as I cycled past a large farmhouse, I spotted a small Jack Russell terrier sitting peacefully in his driveway. I knew as soon as I saw him that he'd also had a turbulent past, interspersed with long periods of aching dullness. He resented the intrusion of a passing cyclist into his tranquil afternoon, certainly enough to snarl and snap at my heels and pursue me for half a mile up the road. It was the first time that I had been chased by a dog during my trip and I wasn't sure whether it was best

to get off and threaten or pedal like fury. Inevitably, I chose the latter
– not so good at calming
animals.

Kelso Abbey

My plan to head for
Kirk Yetholm and stay at the
Youth Hostel was foiled as
there was no answer when I
rang to book in advance.
Rather than risk arriving to
find another full hostel, I
decided to stay on the main
tourist route and headed for
Kelso instead. The border
turns south at Coldstream,
away from the river Tweed,
to link up with the high ridges
of the Cheviot Hills that form
the largest natural barrier between England and Scotland. The only
crossing routes through this mountain range that avoid high ground
are at the coastal plains by Berwick and Gretna. The one high route
into Scotland, the A68, crosses the Cheviots at Carter Bar at a height
of 1370 feet. With this one exception, these hills have remained
largely unchallenged by the Romans and traffic planners. I kept on the
main road along the Tweed valley all the way to the market town of
Kelso where I nearly fell off my bike again, this time on the wet
cobbled streets. I was surprised at how beautiful a place it was, its
open town square surrounded by proud old buildings, reminiscent of
the centre of some French towns. Nearby are the arches and high
columns of the ruined abbey and, on the west side of this royal burgh,
the bridge used as the model design for London Bridge. There was a
fine sunset later that evening offering beautiful views along the river
Tweed and across to the turrets of Floors Castle.

Kelso to Newcastleton

I was awake early, keen to get out on the road again and felt good and surprisingly fit – for the first mile of the day. I soon began to slow down on the eleven miles to Jedburgh, rueing the excesses of a yet another cooked breakfast. I stopped at the Teviot Water Gardens and relaxed by the side of the streams which wind their way down through the rocks and banks of hostas and marigolds and the stillness of the lily ponds. Back on the road again, the slight head wind provided some excuse for my feeble progress. The land was flat and I needed to feel stronger if I were to manage the hill crossing ahead of me later in the day. At Jedburgh, the tiered walls of the Abbey stretch up to the sky like some giant lacework structure towering above the town.

Jedburgh Abbey

Mary Queen of Scots lived here and legend has it that she took a horse and rode alone the twenty-five miles across the Cheviot Hills to visit the injured Bothwell at Hermitage Castle near Newcastleton. Even these days, it is a lonely route, described by a local as the 'road to nowhere'. I certainly encountered very few people along this isolated border crossing. A harsher landscape emerges as the road leaves the rolling hills and farmlands around Bonchester Bridge for the long climb up through the Wauchope Forest. Now I understood why this part of the Borders, known as the 'Debatable Lands', was ungovernable for so many centuries. It had been disowned at times by both Scotland and England and was home to the anarchy of the border reivers. When the two kingdoms were not clashing over the territory, local feuds filled up their spare time and the mosstroopers – now there's a good name for a rugby club – took control of the hills. By the fourteenth century, a special form of administration was set up to try and control the lawlessness of the cattle thieves and murderers. Leaders of local families were appointed as Wardens on both sides of the Anglo-Scottish frontier, each responsible for a section of the border – the three Marches, the West, Middle and East. More destruction was to follow in the sixteenth century when, at the orders of Henry VIII, much of the Scottish side of the border was ravaged and the abbeys of Kelso and Jedburgh, Melrose and Dryburgh were left in ruins. Nowadays, the land of the mosstroopers is cloaked in trees, herringbone rows of pines stretching across the hills for as far as the eye can see.

The warm day and fine views across the surrounding farmlands kept me going on a slow pedal up onto those hills, on the B6357 across to Liddesdale. The sense of remoteness grew and one of the few houses I passed had a golden eagle on the lawn. Brakes screeched. That couldn't have been a golden eagle? Yes, there it was, perched on a tree stump behind three peregrine falcons. I had just spotted the two enormous eagle owls by the hedge when the owner came out with yet another bird of prey perched on his gloved hand. Each bird was tethered to a white stand and the falconer explained that these were used as bases for the parasols which were put up to shield the birds from the heat of the summer sun. It must be a slightly bizarre sight for passing drivers. I resumed my uphill journey, occasionally looking up into the clear blue skies, hoping to see an eagle or even a red kite, with or without umbrellas.

The forested hills on the road to Newcastleton

At last I reached the top of the pass over the hills, at the Note O' the Gate, some 1250 feet up on Fanna Hill. From there, it was a rapid descent through a rockier landscape on this side of the hills, past Saughtree and Larriston and down into Liddesdale, its wild meadows sprinkled with buttercups. I half expected the remote village of Newcastleton, where I had booked accommodation in advance, to be a rather closed community. It was good, therefore, to find relaxed smiles for strangers. I cycled across to look at nearby Hermitage Castle, which, even on a summer's evening, still looked severe and forbidding. A bleak fortress, built to survive the ravages of some of the worst of the Border warfare, Hermitage Castle is said to have been rebuilt following the collapse of its walls when they could no longer support the weight of iniquity! Not much cheer here for Mary at the end of her ride: a wild place where even the hermits huddled together for safety!

Newcastleton to Dumfries

Liddesdale looked beautiful in the warm sunshine as I cruised down the valley, setting out on the fifty-mile cycle to Dumfries. Just before Canonbie, the land drops away steeply, opening up views across to the west and in the distance I could just make out a wide expanse of pale, flat land. Then I realised that I was looking over to the tidal estuary of the Solway Firth. For two and a half days since leaving Berwick, I knew that, as long as I kept going, I would reach the sea again. Nevertheless, it was a surprise to catch sight of the water beyond the tidal mud. That first glimpse of distant sea never fails to excite.

Border landscape from Bonchester Bridge

Shortly after entering the Dumfries and Galloway region, the B6357 crosses the River Esk at Canonbie, a prosperous looking village with an old coach inn, the Cross Keys. You could almost hear the contented clucking sound in the lazy warmth of the mid-morning sunshine as the villagers went about their business. From here, I briefly joined the A7 to Longtown, following alongside the waters of the River Esk on its way down to the Solway Firth. The Esk marked the border between England and Scotland until 1552 when a three-and-a-half-mile earthwork, known as Scots Dike, was constructed to the west, joining up with the River Sark north of Gretna and marking the new frontier. This is the only part of the border where there is no obvious natural barrier of mountain or river and the area is said to have known 'no other thing but theft, reiff, and slaughter' until the new boundary was finally agreed. At Longtown, I headed west along the A6071 before dipping under the roar of the A74 trunk road traffic to arrive in Gretna.

It is possible to walk along the shore from here to Annan and I was hopeful of finding the former Loch and Dornock Fisheries' road along the shore. A policeman gave me directions for Redkirk and from here I found a track that led down to the shore. However, the route disappeared amongst the rocks along the beach and I had to carry the bike for several hundred yards before I could reach the grassy foreshore. Although I could push it over the grass, this was still no way to travel any distance. So, despite the fine location, I began to look for an escape path heading inland. At low tide the waters of the Solway Firth are reduced to a narrow stream where the River Esk carves its route through the mud flats close to the Solway Firth's northern shore. I stopped for a while to watch two men standing motionless in the middle of the stream, each carrying on his shoulders shortened goal posts with the net still attached. It only took me about ten minutes to realise that they were fishing: the net and no sign of a ball eventually gave it away, and I concluded that they were the salmon fishers who trawl these waters on foot. A little later, they were joined by a third goalkeeper who appeared to have walked all the way across the Solway Firth from Cumbria. Apparently, there are several fords or 'waths' that can be used as tracks across the waters of the Solway between England and Scotland. The best-known one is the crossing between the Roman fort at Bowness in Cumbria over the estuary to Annan, a route that would make for a bold cycle route on another day. It became obvious that I should have had a closer look at the maps when planning my coastal route because this all too brief stretch of off-road cycling, more of a shore stumble, had to be abandoned shortly afterwards. I returned to the tarmac for the last few miles to Annan.

Once a shipbuilding town where buccaneers 'ran contraband up the Solway, despite the efforts of excisemen', including Robert Burns, Annan appears to have had a lively past. Outliving a curse placed upon it by St Malachy O'Moore in 1149, for a long time it was the centre of fierce border feuding and slaughter. I left the town and cycled down the minor roads through Powfoot and Cummertrees before reaching Ruthwell where the world's first savings bank was established. I mention this detail as if it were of some importance to me. But, no! I completely ignored the village savings bank museum, wondering only as I passed, whether somewhere in Britain at this very moment, some earnest financial historian was laying plans for the birthplace of the Personal Equity Plan. Even though I had come across a book devoted entirely to the magnificence of the seventh century Ruthwell Cross in the village church, I didn't stop to see that either. Instead, I lay down and slept in a nearby hayfield, lulled by the smell of the freshly-cut grass.

The noise of the approaching bailer disturbed my rural reverie and I got up quickly to avoid a haystack haircut. The skies had become overcast but it was still warm and sticky and the cycling was easy going across flat farmland countryside. At Bankend, the B725 doubles back on itself and heads down to the marshes of the Solway coast where the dignified towers and sandstone walls of Caerlaverock Castle stand proudly above the still waters of the surrounding moat. On the opposite bank of the river Nith, the steep slopes of Criffell mountain rose up from the coastal plain to dominate the skyline of the northern shore of the Solway Firth. As I headed northwards again towards Dumfries, a mouse ran across the road, its tiny legs a blur of frantic activity. Nearby, a couple of salmon fishermen stood still-as-herons in the river mud.

I arrived in Dumfries at half-past-five and the town seemed hot, noisy and intolerant. Fortunately, the person in the tourist office turned out to be helpful, arranging some good accommodation and directing me to a bicycle shop in town. It was closed, but it was kindly opened up to give me yet another bolt for the loose cycle rack. The River Nith and the memory of Robert Burns flow through the centre and I spent some time wandering round the town, ending up at the cemetery where Burns is buried alongside his Jean. They share a very smart white mausoleum set amongst a tumbled-down busy little graveyard where a red sandstone memorial sculpture and leaning headstones commemorate the passing of many local dignitaries.

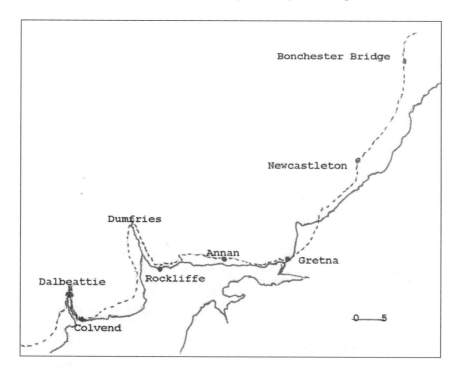

Dumfries to Gatehouse of Fleet

I woke up to the sound of heavy rain and when I drew back the curtains it proved to be even worse than it sounded. An early breakfast at 7.45 now didn't seem such a good idea and it was nearly ten o'clock before I was packed and wrapped sufficiently to begin pedalling. By now, the rain was even heavier and the landlady declared me mad to go out in it. She was probably right, for within a few miles, every crevice of my clothing was wet. I had taken the precaution of tying some rather elegant looking plastic bags round my socks to keep out the worst of the spray from the road to no avail, and my shoes began to top up with water. With the wind behind me, I didn't feel too cold despite that watery feeling moving from all directions towards my saddled crotch.

I was heading south on the A710 main road across Whinny Hill, before descending to the village of New Abbey. The red walls of ruined Sweetheart Abbey rose up from a floor of bright green lawn and brought some welcome colour to the gloom of the day. I had hoped to climb Criffell to enjoy the reportedly magnificent views along the whole length of the Solway coast. When even the foot of the hill was in thick mist, I had no choice but to peddle on past Kirkbean where Paul Jones, pirate and founder of The United States Navy, was born, and on to Sandyhills Bay on the coast. Progress was good and the roadside grasses, bent westwards in the wind, waved me on.

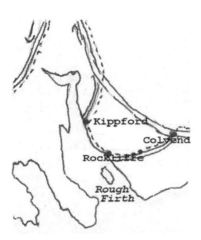

At Colvend, I took a narrow side road to the left that drops down to the sea at Rockcliffe where a small cluster of houses with attractive gardens runs down to the rocky shore. From the village, I followed a route for two miles through the forest across Mark Hill, and joined up with the Jubilee Path on the other side of the headland. Once out of the trees, the path follows the coast, past decorative houses and sculptures of animals made from pieces of gnarled driftwood, to the small port of Kippford. I had heard that it was possible to take a boat across the estuary at certain times of the year but the man in the ship's chandlers was quick to point out that this wasn't one of them, and no, he didn't have any watertight bags for my feet. I cycled on to the small private 'Keep Out' pier to glance briefly at the banks of grey mud exposed by the departed tide before heading back inland.

The rain had relented when I reached Dalbeattie and I became more cheerful as I began to dry out. From here, the road steers clear of the coast and climbs on to rolling hills before dropping down into the village of Dundrennan, tucked into a fold in the hills. I should have stopped to look at the ruined abbey, but tiredness and the prospect of stopping for the night kept me pedalling across the hills. It was lonely up there with little traffic to disturb the gloom of the afternoon. Then the puncture! This time I heard it, a staccato hiss, if that is not a contradiction in terms. I was able to start cursing even before I felt the judder of the front wheel rumbling along the tarmac. Anger and anxiety immediately replaced the tiredness as I stopped to peel off the tyre and look for the cause of the blow out. This time, I had the sense to check the outer tyre. Sure enough, the wall had split as well and the inner tube was bulging out and scraping the brake blocks.

It was a fraught few miles to Kircudbright, mainly downhill and without front brakes. Much relieved, I found a cycle shop in the town where I bought the appropriate tyre for my mountain bike. Repairs completed, I relaxed and enjoyed a leisurely pedal around the town, looking at a range of architectural styles, including fine Georgian houses, a seventeenth century church-like Tolbooth and the castle by the river. Then it was time to make the short trip over the hills to Gatehouse of Fleet.

Gatehouse of Fleet to Port William

Nestling amongst the hills and surrounded by woodlands, it is difficult to believe that this small village of neat, whitewashed houses was once the centre of a thriving cotton textile industry in Galloway. Like many other 'coastal' Solway towns, it lies a few miles inland, tucked away at the end of a small bay and the only route westwards was to follow the main A75 trunk road along the coast to Creetown and on to Newton Stewart. With the help of a following wind, I covered the eighteen miles to Newton Stewart in one hour and twenty minutes. At fourteen miles an hour, this is still slower than even half the speed that a Tour de France rider might take to cover a hundred miles or so. However, it was good going for me.

Gatehouse of Fleet

Now on the penultimate peninsula of my journey round Scotland, I headed south on the main A174 road to Wigtown, the

capital of this isolated shire. Despite deserving attention, I barely
slowed to admire the broad town square of Newton Stewart. The
morning mist had cleared and I was very hot and exhausted by the
time I arrived in Whithorn, a dignified if somewhat severe looking
town with a wide and sombre main street. I found a cafe with a table
set outside on the pavement to enjoy the warmth of the mid-afternoon
sunshine. The bill was only a pound for a slice of cake and a cup of
coffee, a far cry from central Scotland prices. In fact, the whole
peninsula has a remote feeling about it. Largely ignored by passing
tourists, it had once been a Mecca for the early Christian missionaries.
St Ninian is thought to have founded the first Christian centre in
Scotland here and layers of history, dating back to the fifth century,
are being uncovered by archaeologists in the town. Although remote
for overland routes, the sea crossings between the Celtic tribes of
Ireland, Scotland, Wales and from as far south as Brittany, made this
part of the Solway coast a centre of pilgrimage in medieval Europe. I
marvelled at the extent of the excavations in the middle of the town
and was left wondering where all the topsoil that buried the walls had
come from. I made my way back to the coast, visiting the protective
ring of low houses around the busy harbour of the seaside village of
the Isle of Whithorn.

   After a brief stop in the village, I set out to follow the
Pilgrim's way around Burrow Head to reach St Ninian's Cave on the
other side of the headland. I had been looking forward to this off-road
section since reading about the pioneering work of Andrew Patterson,
a local minister, who has been promoting a 'Pilgrim Way' along the
Solway coast. A local leaflet seemed to confirm that a route 'for
walking, riding and cycling' could be followed round Burrow Head. I
had some difficulty finding the beginning of the pilgrimage way as
there was little evidence of route markings. Following a track across a
field, it soon became obvious that it crossed ground that was too soft
for cycling. There was also a large bull roaming free on the other side
of the field, so, with a righteous mixture of conservation and self-
preservation, I reluctantly decided to retreat. When I got back to the
road, I met the local farmer leaning on the gate. He had been watching

my progress with some interest and growing rage. His welcoming words of legal retribution indicated that some of the negotiations with local landowners on the exact route of the Pilgrim's Way were far from complete. Following suitable apologies, grovelling might be a better description, we parted amicably enough, me to the tarmac and he to more pilgrim watching. My enthusiasm to visit the cave which St Ninian is said to have used as a retreat, was waning and, as grey clouds gathered overhead, I took the main A747 road through Glasserton. A sea mist had descended, followed by a light drizzle by the time I arrived in Port William. On a grey evening, this grey town looked kind of … grey.

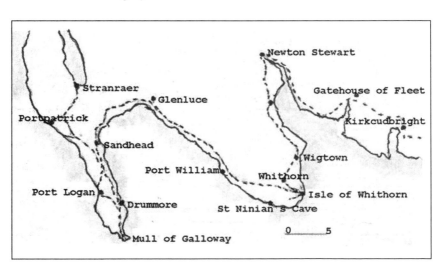

Port William to Portpatrick

ort William had even less colour in the morning and I was glad
to escape from my tiny room in the B&B and along the coast
road towards Glenluce. I was heading into a strong breeze and
progress was slow with only hazy views, across Luce Bay, to the
flattened strip of the Mull of Galloway to relieve the grind. It was a
relief to reach Glenluce, and turn south again, feeling the wind at my
back as I entered my last peninsula, the Rhins of Galloway. Now I
was able to pedal faster, ducking low beneath two giant Chinook

helicopters that reared up from
behind a hedge to circle
menacingly overhead. At last I
really believed that I would
reach Portpatrick and my
excitement grew with the rattle
of gunfire and the flash of
flares as these 'Vietnam'
helicopters swooped down
across the bay on their assault
flight.

The cliffs at the Mull of Galloway

The landscape here is
varied, the road passing by the
sleepy village of Sandhead,
around quiet bays and through
woodlands before emerging on the high barren ground beyond
Drummore. From here, the route down to the Mull crosses green and
empty hills with open views over the sea into the grey distance of an
imagined shape of Ireland. At last, the never-ending strip of tarmac
heading south to the Mull began to descend to where the bays of East
and West Tarbert almost meet before rising up for a final climb onto

the rocky headland on the most southerly point of Scotland. Dark clouds and cold, unforgiving winds added to the grandeur of this final headland. I walked across to the lighthouse perched on top of the Mull and along the narrow paths which scrape the very edge of the steep cliffs. The sheer walls of rock are splashed with yellow lichen and sea pinks. I found a place to shelter from the wind and look down the plunging rocks to the waters of the Irish Sea far below.

I was reluctant to leave, thoughtful of the twenty hilly miles into a northerly headwind ahead of me. It took me some time to waterproof-up in the car park, watched closely by half a dozen people huddled round their thermos cups in the warmth of their cars, smiling in sympathy at me. Well I think it was sympathy showing through the sweaty windscreens, but perhaps it was dismay at the sight of a blue vision of crumpled inelegance. Apart from a fire-proof inner suit, I had the lot on – pullover, fleecy, waterproof trousers, cagoule, gloves and helmet. I could barely move. Even the simple act of getting my leg over the saddle almost proved a straddle too far.

Logan Botanic Gardens near Port Logan

It was a slow cycle back north, past East Tarbert to Damnaglaur where I took the B7065 to the village of Port Logan. There is a fine stretch of beach here and a famous fish-pond which, at high tide, traps fish from the sea in an inland pool. The main attraction is the beautiful Logan Botanic Gardens, a specialist part of the Royal Botanic Garden Edinburgh. Warmed by the Gulf Stream and sheltered by banks of trees and high walls, it has an exotic display of cabbage, palm trees and water gardens, magnolias, tree ferns and Chusan palms. Or so the brochure says, and it certainly looked as impressive as it sounds, with smooth lawns and regimented planting designs providing a striking contrast to the surrounding countryside. It was certainly a good place to escape from the wind for an hour or so.

Back pedalling again up what seemed to be never-ending hills, I reached the village of Ardwell. It was now after five o'clock and, with still twelve miles to go, I tried to book ahead some accommodation in Portpatrick. I was very impressed to find a room in Melvin Lodge, the first place I telephoned. I was even more impressed when the owner offered to come and meet me. This seemed to be taking customer care even further than I thought possible. (I later discovered that when I told him that I was arriving by bike, he miss-heard this as 'by boat' and was offering to walk the fifty or so yards down to the pier to meet me!) Anyway, having cycled this far, I declined his kind offer although I began to regret it as the evening and I wore slowly on, both becoming increasingly grey. The wind still refused to ease and the mileage signposts were miserly with their encouragement until at last I reached that sign which said 'Portpatrick'. Then, in a blink of an eye, there was 'splendour, splendour everywhere' and I felt all the exhilaration of a champion as I rolled down that hill, down to the sea.

That night, tucked away in the snug bar of a Portpatrick pub, I mulled over the journey. In thirty-five days of cycling, covering anything from twenty cross-country miles to seventy miles on long, tarmac days, I had circled the edge of Scotland. I had pedalled some fifteen hundred miles, the equivalent of Edinburgh to Barcelona, or Lands End to John o' Groats and nearly back again. Impressed? No, not when you discover that the record time for cycling from Lands End to John o' Groats is held by a man who took just one day and twenty-one hours. He could have completed this jaunt in less than four days and I had taken four and a half years. Mind you, he probably didn't stop to look at the views.

I contemplated the changes to the coastline that have taken place since I started out in October 1992. Two of the ferry routes, across the Kyles of Lochalsh and the Cromarty Firth have closed. Lighthouses have been automated and all are now silent. No more conversations with the keepers at Cape Wrath, no washing hung out at Dunnet Head, no sound of life at St Abb's Head or the Mull of Galloway: nothing except the cry of the sea birds! 'The whole coast is going completely blind,' the principal keeper at Fair Isle South said when the last of Scotland's lighthouses was automated. The sea level has risen and is expected to rise each year (up to twenty centimetres over the next fifty years) so that parts of the Solway coast, the Dornoch Firth and the area around the Tentsmuir Forest might disappear altogether.

While I will not miss some of the pedalling, those winter evenings spent planning and pouring over maps will be a loss. It was very satisfying to confirm for myself that all the separate pieces of the country's jigsaw really do fit together. Even the rail links, despite the hassle of travelling with a bicycle, have been fun. Low moods, nearly always brought on by tiredness and lack of food, are over-shadowed by so many high points, not least the simple sense of feeling grown-up enough at fifty to travel on my own and the folly of pretending to myself for a few days each year that I was free. Somehow, being alone heightens senses and lifts the soul. Or perhaps it is just the heart rate? And then the sun setting over the Cuillins and daybreak at Sandwood Bay and …

Postscard from Barcelona

It is now almost ten years since that evening in October when I cycled out of Portpatrick on the road to Stranraer. Not only did it take me four years to complete my coastal cycle, but writing up the journey proved to be an even slower pastime. And a lot has happened for cyclists since 1992. Judging by the increasing number of cars these days with bicycle racks strapped precariously to their tails, cycling is growing in popularity. Certainly the government hopes so and is aiming to double the number of cyclists on the roads in the next ten years.

There is also now no shortage of information on cycle routes. *Sustrans* publishes detailed maps on the National Cycle Network with much of the east coast covered by 'National Route 1' which runs close to the sea all the way from John o 'Groats to Edinburgh. The Cycle Touring Club (CTC) provides route plans for much of the west coast and there are several locally produced leaflets on off-road cycle routes. These include Fife's information leaflet on their 'Millennium Cycleways' and Forest Enterprise's booklet on 'Cycling in the Borders'.

Some of the landmarks have changed as well. Planes now land at Prestwick Airport and those 'mini oil platforms' at the Kyle of Lochalsh have been built up to form the Skye Bridge. Edinburgh has finally noticed that it has a waterfront, launching a variety of buildings – office blocks, hotels and even an 'Ocean Terminal' shopping mall to prove it. Ownership of the land in some of the more remote areas of the west coast has also changed. Parts of Assynt, the island of Eigg and more recently, the Knowdart Estate and Gigha are owned and managed by local communities.

Tourist facilities for cyclists have improved. In some places, bar meals are now available after nine o'clock. Many Youth Hostels, including Oban, have been upgraded although, sadly, some have been closed. Independent hostels and bunkhouses are on the increase throughout the country. ScotRail is more accommodating about carrying bikes and information on rail/ferry links is more easily available. And for those wishing to cycle the Western Isles, holders of Caledonian MacBrayne's Island Hopscotch ® tickets can take bicycles free.

Once I had discovered that my piece of string for measuring the map distance around Scotland would also stretch to Barcelona, I resumed my winter planning evenings. On a warm but wet Saturday morning last October, I pedalled into the Placa de Catalunya on my first visit to this beautiful city. On this occasion, I really cheated, chopping off most of the string by flying to Carcassonne and then cycling over one of last year's Tour de France 'category one' climbs in the Pyrenees. My wheels actually rolled over Ullrich's name, writ large across the tarmac: a day to realise childhood dreams even though my three-hour halting climb of 3000 feet had been covered by Jan in just fifty minutes. There again, he didn't have the baggage! Then it was down the Costa Brava coastline – and sunshine.

Even so, when it comes to shorelines, Scotland's west coast is hard to beat.

A Note on the History of Scotland

As the 'mists of antiquity' began to clear, the Romans left Britain to the next wave of invaders, the Angles and Saxons. They pushed the Celtic Britons out to the fringes – Cornwall, Wales, Northumbria and as far north as Strathclyde. By about 650AD, Scotland was populated by four different peoples. The Picts occupied the north-east from Caithness down to the Forth, the Angles were already opening shops in Morningside and outlying districts, and the Britons were in Strathclyde. Argyll, or Dalriada, as it was then known, was being occupied by the Scots, a Gaelic-speaking people from the North of Ireland.

Norse raiders appeared in the late eighth century and subsequently seized the western and northern isles. Although the Scots and the Picts were joined in 843 under Kenneth McAlpin, king of the Scots of Dalriada, it wasn't until 1034 that his descendant, Duncan, became king of all Scotland. He was killed in battle by Macbeth and there then followed a succession of Scottish kings, often engaged in border warfare with England, until in 1296, Edward I succeeded in 'conquering' Scotland for the time being. William Wallace, a Scottish knight, provided a focus for resistance to English rule, a role taken over by Robert the Bruce. In 1314, the battle at Bannockburn took place when the army of Edward II was routed.

More kings and border battles followed over the next two centuries as the House of Stewart ruled Scotland through a succession of Roberts and Jameses. The Highland clans kept their fierce independence with many retaining allegiance to the Lords of the Isles and ignoring the Scottish crown.

In 1513, the 'Auld Alliance' with France, based on shared conflicts with the English, resulted in the Scottish army becoming involved disastrously in a 'European' war leading to defeat and the death of James IV at Flodden. The English King, Henry VIII, now sought to control a weakened Scotland. In 1542, the week-old Mary Queen of Scots succeeded her father, James V, to the Scottish throne. When the Scots decided against Henry's ploy of a marriage between Mary and his son, Henry's army invaded Scotland. He found allies amongst the divided Highlands by taking advantage of the split between Protestantism, preached by John Knox, and Catholicism which had its links with France.

After an early childhood spent sheltering in various castles throughout Scotland, and a number of years in France, Catholic Mary returned to Scotland to find that she was on 'the wrong side'. Two unsuccessful marriages and religious differences eventually led to her abdication and flight to England. Her baby son remained in Scotland and was crowned King James VI in 1567. Mary was held prisoner for nearly twenty years before her execution at the order of her cousin, Elizabeth I. When Elizabeth died, James succeeded her, becoming James I of Great Britain.

The English Civil War, Cromwell and the reigns of Charles I and II passed by before the last 'legitimate' Scottish monarch, King James VII and II, took flight in 1688 before the armies of William of Orange. Whilst the Scottish parliament recognized William and his daughter, Mary, as king and queen of Scotland, there was still strong support for James in the Highlands. William sent troops to subdue these 'Jacobites', building garrisons at Fort William and Fort Augustus. The major events of William's campaign to subdue the rebellious Highlanders were the battle at Killiecrankie and the notorious massacre at Glencoe.

The signing of the unpopular Treaty of Union in 1707, whereby Scotland lost its parliament, angered Scots who wished to retain their separate sovereignty. A permanent military presence under General Wade was established to police the Highlands, building roads to improve military communications. In 1745, the grandson of James VII, 'Bonnie Prince Charlie', arrived from France to claim his Scottish crown. Initially successful, his forces were eventually slaughtered at Culloden. He was hunted as a fugitive across the Highlands and Islands before fleeing to France. Those Highlanders who had supported Charlie paid dearly for this; the clan system was dismantled and land divided up into estates. The profitability of these estates relied on the introduction of sheep farming and landlords evicted tenants in the savage Clearances of the late eighteenth and early nineteenth centuries. The Clearances, widespread emigration and the shift of population towards the emerging industrial centres in the south, left a Scotland divided into the sparsely-peopled Highlands and the relatively prosperous central belt.

The most recent significant political development took place in July 1999 when the Scottish Parliament came into being once again.

Sources of information

Cycling and Cycle routes

Sustrans Information Service, Scotland, Tel 0131 624 7660 or 01179 290 888
Website www.sustrans.org.uk
Visit Scotland's 'Cycling Scotland'. Website www.visitscotland.com
Cyclists Touring Club (CTC), Tel 08708 730 060. Website www.ctc.org.uk

Ferries for Cyclists

Caledonian MacBrayne offers a range of ferry routes that allows cyclists to explore the west coast of Scotland. Most mainland ferry terminals have good rail links. Bicycles are permitted on all ferries. With 'Island Hopscotch' ® tickets for combining several island or peninsula crossings, bicycles are carried free of charge. Website www.calmac.co.uk

Bibliography -The Scottish Coastal Areas

Murray, W H: *The Companion Guide to the West Highlands of Scotland* (Collins)
Atkinson, Tom: *Empty Lands* (Luath Press)
Smith, Robert: *One Foot in the Sea* (John Donald Publishers Ltd)
Blake, Brian: *The Solway Firth* (Robert Hale London)

Bibliography - The British Coastline

Raban, Jonathan: *Coasting* (Collins Harvill)
Scale, Evans, McLean: *Walking Britain's Coast* (Unwin Hyman)
Merrill, John: *Turn Right at Land's End* (Walk and Write Ltd)
Theroux, Paul: *The Kingdom by the Sea* (Hamish Hamilton/Penguin Books)

Bibliography – Other Reference Books

Morton, H V: *In Scotland Again* (Methuen)
Johnson, Samuel: *A Journey to Western Isles of Scotland* (Chapman & Dodd)
Maclean, Fitzroy: *A Concise History of Scotland* (Thames and Hudson)
Dunning, Mercer, Owen, Roberts & Lambert: *Britain before Man* (HMSO)
Sissons, J B: *The Evolution of Scotland's Scenery* (Oliver & Boyd)
Stewart, Arthur: *Long Distance Walks in Scotland* (Crowood)

Cualann Press Titles

Of Fish and Men: Tales of a Scottish Fisher
David C Watson
Foreword: Derek Mills
ISBN 0 9535036 3 1 ... Price £10.99

In Search of Willie Patterson
A Scottish Soldier in the Age of Imperialism
Fred Reid
ISBN 09535036 7 4 ... Price £10.99

The Lion and the Eagle: Reminiscences of Polish Second World War Veterans in Scotland
Editor: Dr Diana M Henderson LLB TD FSA Scot.
Foreword: His Excellency Dr Stanislaw Komorowski
ISBN: 0 9535036 4 X ... £9.99

Stand By Your Beds! A Wry Look at National Service
David Findlay Clark OBE, MA,, Ph.D., C.Psychol., F.B.Ps.S.
Preface: Trevor Royle, historian and writer
ISBN: 0 9535036 6 6 ... £13.99

Open Road to Faraway: Escapes from Nazi POW Camps 1941-1945
Andrew Winton D A (Edin)
Foreword: Allan Carswell, Curator, National War Museum of Scotland
ISBN: 0 9535036 5 8 ... £9.99

Beyond the Bamboo Screen: Scottish Prisoners of War under the Japanese
Extracts from Newsletters of the Scottish Far East Prisoner of War
Association and Other Sources
Tom McGowran OBE. Foreword and Illustrations by G S Gimson QC
ISBN 0 9535036 1 5 ... Price £9.99

On Flows the Tay: Perth and the First World War
Dr Bill Harding Ph.D., FEIS
Foreword: *The Times* journalist and author
ISBN 0 9535036 2 3 ... Price £12.99

Under the Shadow: Letters of Love and War
The Poignant Testimony and Story of Hugh Wallace Mann and Jessie Reid
Foreword: Dr Diana M Henderson
Narrative: Bríd Hetherington
ISBN 0 9535036 0 7 ... Price £12.99

Cualann Press: Email cualann@btinternet.com Website www.cualann.co.uk